Where You Stand Is Where You Sit

OTHER BOOKS BY ROBERT V. SMITH

Development & Management of University Research Groups

Graduate Research: A Guide for Students in the Sciences

The Elements of Great Speechmaking: Adding Drama & Intrigue

Pedestals, Parapets & Pits: The Joys, Challenges & Failures of Professional Life

Where You Stand Is Where You Sit

An Academic Administrator's Handbook

ROBERT V. SMITH

with *Illustrations by Dusty Higgins*

The University of Arkansas Press

FAYETTEVILLE ■ 2006

10   09   08   07   06   5   4   3   2   1

ISBN-10: cloth = 1-55728-829-1
          paper = 1-55728-830-5
ISBN 13: cloth = 975-1-55728-829-5
          paper = 975-1-55728-830-1

Text design by Ellen Beeler

Library of Congress Cataloging-in-Publication Data

Smith, Robert V.
  Where you stand is where you sit : an academic administrator's handbook / Robert V. Smith.
     p. cm.
  Includes bibliographical references and index.
  ISBN 1-55728-829-1 (casebound : alk. paper) — ISBN 1-55728-830-5 (pbk. : alk. paper)
  1. Education, Higher—Administration—Handbooks, manuals, etc.
  2. Educational leadership—Handbooks, manuals, etc. I. Title.
  LB2341.S65 2006
  378.1'11—dc22

                                                     2006019215

To my muse, the Daughter of Mars

Disclaimer

This book strictly reflects the independent scholarship and views of the author. Unless very specifically noted otherwise, nothing portrayed in this work should be construed as the official policy or position of any institution where the author has worked or is currently employed.

Contents

Section III. Guidance to Various Academic Administrators and Support Professionals

Epilogue   189

Preface

American Colleges and Universities prepare a large proportion of the leaders and major participants in the worlds of business, industry, government, and the learned professions but do little to prepare their own faculty members (and eventual administrators) for the world of higher education. . . . In many cases, faculty members can barely see beyond their own discipline or narrow specialization, viewing even that as independent of their own campus issues. The time and place to change this pattern are in the preparation of the professoriate and through the provision of professional outlets for faculty members' continued development as academic citizens.

—MILTON GREENBERG (1927–), emeritus professor, provost, and interim president, American University

"Where you stand is where you sit." It's an old aphorism that rings true across many sectors of society. In higher education particularly, it suggests that your position in an academic institution helps shape your views—be they related to personnel or program development, philosophic perspective, or policies. For academic higher-education administrators, including provosts and vice-presidents or vice-chancellors, deans and directors, department chairs and heads, and administrative support professionals and administrative assistants, the level and scope of responsibilities certainly influence perspectives. Yet, there are elements of common understanding of the higher-education enterprise that all academic administrators ought to possess to ensure professional success and advancement. Such common understanding is at the heart of this work.

I have served for more than thirty years in academic administrative posts at four public research universities (i.e., the University of Arkansas, University of Connecticut, University of Texas at Austin, and Washington State University). The journey has included appointments as academic division head; assistant director, associate director and director of a research institute; dean of a professional college; dean of two graduate schools; interim dean of an honors college; chief research officer (vice-provost) at two institutions; and chief academic officer (provost and vice-chancellor for academic affairs). While I cannot claim to "have seen it all," the breadth of responsibilities and experiences I have had are wide and rich. Thinking back, I can now imagine how I would have valued having the work you currently hold in your hands. Indeed, as you scan its table of contents and flip through its pages, I believe you will identify with the topics and text—some familiar, some less familiar.

This handbook emanates from a set of communication strategies I crafted during the past twenty years of my administrative life and had its origin in a somewhat negative experience. Years ago, I had a supervisor who had a reputation for not communicating well with members of his unit. In fact, a direct report was once heard to say, "communicating with that guy is like sending missives to the dead-letter section of the post office." My attempts to avoid getting such a reputation involved not only a dedication to being a responsive e-mail correspondent but also the development and use of communication vehicles including a magazine, newsletters, and in more recent years, a quarterly on-line journal, *All Things Academic* (*ATA*), through which I have shared thoughts on university policies, planning, and philosophical perspectives. I have been the sole author of many articles and other pieces in *ATA*, but some involved collaborative efforts with other administrative colleagues. Indeed, the authoring of work with direct reports is—in and of itself—an excellent communication and morale-building strategy.

The content of *ATA* over a six-year period suggested a set of overarching topics that have became part of this book. And, while a number of the original *ATA* contributions were previously custom-tailored to the University of Arkansas academic community, I have rewritten and converted several *ATA* articles into chapters that should have broad appeal to administrators in higher education in the United States. Whatever value the articles and this handbook may have for administrative colleagues in the international higher-education community is for others to judge.

Besides the communication-related topics noted above and in the table of contents, this handbook is more or less subdivided along the lines of the three main functions of key academic officers, especially provosts, deans, and, to some extent, directors: inspiration, evaluation, and representation. To broaden the usefulness of the work, I've added chapters relevant for newcomer orientation and for regulatory compliance. Overall, I have tried to develop material of usefulness to novices and pros alike. If this turns out to be true, then a primary purpose of the book will have been met.

As I indicate throughout this work, diverse perspectives are greatly valued in all that we do in higher education. I have also been inspired through much of my professional life by something known as Carson's Consolation; that is, "There are no complete failures, because people who fail can always be used as bad examples." Thus, all the successes, foibles, and failures in our professional lives are valuable, and I hope readers will share their thoughts by e-mail (bobsmith@uark.edu) or by surface mail. Comments, alternative views, and suggestions are welcome and may be referenced—with permission of course—in future editions.

About Dusty Higgins and
Inclusion of His Cartoons

During my higher-education career, I have had memorable opportunities to observe, and in some cases, become acquainted with cartoonists who created work based on the academic world. For example, during 1978–79 at the University of Texas at Austin, I witnessed the publication of Berkeley Breathed's wonderful strips (i.e., "Academic Waltz") in the *Daily Texan*. The portrayals of President Peter Flawn were particularly remarkable, and Breathed's early work in Austin led eventually to the Pulitzer Prize–winning "Bloom County," which was retired in 1989 but is being resurrected (along with "Academic Waltz") on websites in 2006.

In the eighties, I teamed up with New York cartoonist Sally Blakemore on the production of two editions of a book on the development and management of university research groups (Smith, 1986). Besides aptly illustrating this work, Blakemore's cartoons were subsequently incorporated in many oral presentations—to make points lively and memorable.

While at Washington State University from 1985 to1997, I had the good fortune to meet WSU alumnus Gary Larson, whose career blossomed during much of that time via his award-winning "Far Side" cartoons. Larson was also a WSU commencement speaker during this period and brought the house down with his admonition to students: "Be weird!"

In my most recent encounter in the world of cartoonists, I have come to know and appreciate the work of University of Arkansas alumnus, Dusty Higgins, whose creative efforts enliven this book and an earlier work (Smith, 2005). I chose to collaborate with Higgins for a number of reasons, not least of all, having the opportunity to use his fanciful art in oral presentations related to subjects contained in this work.

And now, Dusty and I make an irresistible offer to readers of *Where You Stand Is Where You Sit*. You have our permission to use the art from this book in oral presentations given for educational purposes. Other uses require written permission through the University of Arkansas Press. But, I hope you will find the materials of this work—cartoons and all—useful in oral communications, which are so critical to success as an academic administrator.

Properly understood and used, Dusty's cartoons can help us all avoid a common criticism of academic administrators: that we take ourselves too seriously! So, in that spirit and with the wish to produce a work of maximum benefit to sitting and world-be academic administrators—the substantive and light-hearted material contained herein is offered to all readers.

Acknowledgments

Many people have contributed to my understanding and perspective on higher-education administration, not counting the authors of many books I have read on the topic. But, the supervisors I have had—the good ones and the not so good ones— the hundreds of people who have reported to me during my administrative career, and the countless others who have shared a thought or a tear have enriched the landscape and helped to shape my outlook and insight. To all who contributed, I offer a metaphorical toast to their counsel, suggestions, and successful careers.

Many professionals were particularly noteworthy for their sage advice and guidance; my list includes (starting from the beginning of my career) Andrew Bartilucci, Eugene Kupchick, and Hugh Luongo (teachers, St. John's University), Joseph Sinsheimer (master's and doctoral mentor, University of Michigan), Joseph Cannon (division head, University of Iowa), James Doluisio (dean, University of Texas at Austin), Thomas George (provost, Washington State University), Mark Emmert (chancellor and provost, University of Connecticut), and John White (chancellor, University of Arkansas). All members of the above list were teachers or supervisors. Colleagues, friends, and direct reports who also significantly influenced my thinking and dedication include Bob Gassert and Clifford Still (Patchogue, New York); Ara Paul (University of Michigan); Keith Guillory and John Rosazza (University of Iowa); Daniel Acosta, Michael Bauza, Patrick Davis, Paul Erhardt, Gerry Fonken, Shirlette Glover-Milton, Lawrence Hurley, Steven Leslie, Irwin "Chet" Lieb, Alfred Martin, Miriam Regnault de Moreno, Bill Sheffield, Elaine Waller, Richard Wilcox, Claire Weinstein, and John Wheeler (University of Texas at Austin); Bill Heller (U.S. Pharmacopeial Convention); Daniel Banes (U.S. Food and Drug Administration); Matthew McDonald McNaught (First Unitarian Church, Austin, Texas); Creed Abell and Odd Steinsland (University of Texas Medical Branch at Galveston); Ross Baldessarini (Harvard University); Howard Lassman (Hoechst-Roussel Pharmaceuticals); Jane Sheridan (Hoffmann-La Roche); Tony Taraska (The Upjohn Company); Jules LaPidus (Council of Graduate Schools); Heather Monroe (Africa America Institute); Tom Rochon and John Yopp (Educational Testing Service); Steve Burkett, Don Dillman, Barbara Harbach, Mack Johnson, Steve Lilly, Rom Markin, Robert Nilan, John Pierce, Bill and Barbara Rayburn, Larry Simonsmeier, and Tim Steury (Washington State University); Gene

Woodruff (University of Washington); Harold Rosen and John Yost (University of Idaho); Philip Austin, Robert Gray, Ilze Krisst, Gerry Maxwell, Sam Pickering, and Gina Smith (University of Connecticut); Gordhan and Jinx Patel (University of Georgia); Kevin Kelly (Van Scoyoc Associates); Les and Betty Sims (Washington, D.C.); Carolyn Allen, Richard Atkinson, Don Bobbitt, Johnetta Cross Brazzell, Carmen Coustaut, David Gearhart, Dan Ferritor, Collis Geren, Richard Hudson, Daniel and Judith Levine, Suzanne McCray, Bob McMath, George and Kat Paulson, Ashok Saxena, Jeff and Carol Shannon, Nancy Talburt, Kathy and Scott Van Laningham, and Doyle Williams (University of Arkansas); Emilio Del Gesso and Davide Vitale (University of Arkansas Center, Rome, Italy); Guido Fabiani (Universita Roma Tre, Rome, Italy); Tom Bruce and David Pryor (University of Arkansas Clinton School of Public Service); Tracie Dungan and Dusty Higgins *(Arkansas Democrat-Gazette);* Charles Francis (IdeaBank); and Cecelia Cancellaro (Idea Architects).

Throughout my professional career, various administrative assistants, secretaries, and program assistants have contributed to my writing efforts, sometimes typing quotes and notes, other times assisting with PowerPoint production or projections. I single out for special commendations Kathie Biondi, Donna Blacker, Karen Broderick, Lynda Carey, Michael Dews, Linda Dizney, Judy Farwell, Doug Miles, Cindy Morley, Judy Okita, Dottie Williams, and Marilyn Wilson.

I leave for last, the person who always comes first in my life—Marsha June Smith—who is much more than wife or helpmate. She is my confidante, my muse, and my unstinting supporter—in all, a person who changed my life forever.

Getting a Good Start

PREAMBLE

Starting any significant academic endeavor is hard work. All of us can relate to our first days of school (from K-12 through graduate school), our first days in one or more academic appointments, and certainly our first opportunities as administrators. But, with some experience, we learn how to "hit the ground running" or as my good friend and colleague Bob McMath notes, "hit the ground listening"—and, once up and running—maintaining strong and positive positions with your supervisor and the people we serve. Following are three chapters that should help the new administrative appointee and perhaps offer some useful thoughts for the more-experienced administrator who may be going from one post to another.

CHAPTER 1

The Promise of
a New Position

I had an almost intolerable awareness that every morning began with infinite promise. Any book may be read, any idea thought, any action taken. Anything that has ever been possible to human beings is possible to most of us every time the clock says six in the morning. On a day no different from the one now breaking, Shakespeare sat down to begin Hamlet.

—RALPH WALDO EMERSON (1803–1882),
American essayist, poet, and philosopher

Beginning a new administrative position offers many promises. Certainly, there is promise for new challenges and opportunities for the new appointee. However, another meaning of "promise" also arises, namely, what can we or should we be promising the people we intend to serve—in a new and special way? Clearly, our colleagues will want to know about our visions and plans for the future. They will desire understanding of our style of operation. They will want to know what promise we offer for their institution and them.

Following are some ideas on making a transition from one post to another—for our purposes, assuming a chair or dean or some other administrative position—perhaps coming from another institution or organization or even from within the same institution. We'll see how preliminary plans and actions can help with transitions, particularly if one of the actions includes the preparation of a paper containing your views of the road ahead and a description of your communication strategies.

Starting with the Interview

The opportunity for a new position begins with the interview. Make it as strong as possible by gathering extensive background information about the new institution and position. The Internet provides powerful tools for getting this job done, from specific information on the institution's or unit's strategic plans and programs to people who may become future colleagues. A powerful adjunct is Google or equivalent image searches to help identify and seal in your mind the names and faces of people you are likely to meet during the interview process.

Make sure that a formal presentation, if required, is well prepared. Avoid reading your remarks. Rather, consider preparing a PowerPoint presentation that prompts comments (Smith, 2004). And, take the opportunity to imbed images of the new unit or institution—as relevant—in the PowerPoint presentation. You may also use PowerPoint technology to share information on programs or units that you have previously led, perhaps with examples of ideas that might be imported into the new position.

During the interview, practice the advice of Harold Rosen, "to seek what others need" through good listening and drawing out the thoughts of others (Smith, 2005). Remember that interviews—especially for administrative posts—are two-way interactions, with opportunities not only to exhibit skills and experiences but also to demonstrate an interest in the needs and aspirations of those you may serve or work with in a new post.

After the interview, be sure to follow up with e-mail notes to key people you met during the process—indicating your gratitude for the opportunity to share some time and perhaps making an additional specific point or two. During my years of interviewing people for administrative posts of varying types, I have found few things more impressive than the simple follow-up note—poignantly demonstrating thoughtfulness and kindness.

Besides the dual promises alluded to above, interviews and the prospects of new posts, especially those at different institutions, offer opportunities to reinvent oneself. Let's consider this next.

The "New You"

You may think it strange, but I have known people to change significant things about themselves going from one post to another. It may be some-

thing seemingly trivial as the pronunciation of one's name—or something more profound. For example, I have known people to change personality upon assuming a new position. One, for example, consciously and purposefully went from a Type A personality to a Type B. In another instance, an individual dramatically changed his speaking style by incorporating touching stories into presentations. The intriguing side to the above-noted transformations is that people in a new location accept the new you as genuine since they are typically unaware of previous faults or less-attractive personality traits.

Capturing the "Promise" in Writing

The transition from one post to another may also be enriched by more formal writing efforts. Politicians are fond of preparing position papers, which outline their views on policy and other matters. The idea of position papers has merit for the nonpolitical professional as well, and I have used the intriguing title of "The Promise of a New Position," in which the dual concept of signaling one's intent is implicit.

Briefly, here is how a "promise of a new position paper" may be developed. Start by describing the various meanings inherent in the word "promise"— as noted previously. Be sure to comment on the position as a meaningful leadership opportunity—an opportunity to help make a differ-ence in the future of the institution being served. While noting the prom-ises you intend to make to the people who report to you—those whom I refer to throughout the book as "direct reports"—describe hopes for the unit you will be serving and the values you will embrace while carrying out your responsibilities.

An example of the beginning of such a paper are the first few lines of the promise paper shared with the university community at the time I assumed the chief academic officer position (provost) at the University of Arkansas (UA): "A provost should serve the academic community by 1) encouraging faculty, student, staff, and program development; 2) evaluat-ing accomplishments; 3) representing accomplishments to the University's constituents—within and outside of our institution—in collaboration with the Chancellor. My *promise* to you is that I will honor these commitments to the best of my ability while ensuring the values of quality, trust, and integrity—in all that I do."

Summarizing to this point, the promise of a new position paper pro-vides the opportunity to offer ideas on roles, responsibilities, and values. Having done that in the initial section of the paper, you should then con-sider providing some insight into your vision and aspirations for the insti-tution. This part is tricky. On the one hand, you have ideas on where you would like for the relevant unit to go (vision), what milestones the vision will require to become reality (goals and objectives), and how it can all be accomplished (action steps and initiatives). But how do you convey these ideas without leaving the impression that you are going to take your col-leagues someplace without their input? A way to avoid this negative assess-ment is to pose a set of hypothetical questions that provide clues to your thinking without your being perceived as getting too far out in front of the people you will be serving.

For example, the new dean for a professional college might pose ques-tions such as

- What is the current mission for our college?
- How might the mission be expanded to improve the college's con-tributions to the institution and society?
- Are there efficiencies that might be developed to assist an expanded mission?
- If we expand our mission, what information technology infra-structure will be needed to ensure our college's success?

The questions should be customized according to your current understanding of the unit. However, the use of questions signals that you do not have all the answers, and that you will be seeking answers through the unit's faculty members, students, and staff.

The question portion of the paper can be used to segue into a section on ideas of how the answers and further information will be gathered. Here, you can signal an intent to meet with individuals and groups after you have read previous planning documents and reports that may pertain to the future operations of the unit. You should also consider coupling these approaches with a preliminary outline of your anticipated communication strategies.

In the case I alluded to above, I expanded my pledge to the UA community as follows: "As we go forward, we need to remember that a provost can do little without the collaboration and cooperation of all who are served. Thus, a set of communication strategies and follow-through steps will be necessary to serve our goals and objectives. Accordingly, I have planned the following: 1) visits to colleges and schools—all eight of them; 2) follow-up visits to departments (all fifty of them) within colleges and schools in addition to other units that serve the institution's academic mission (e.g., Office of Institutional Research, the Libraries); 3) regular contact with faculty, students, and staff; 4) creation of a web-based journal; 5) development of all-campus forums to engage our community in issues of broad academic interest." The visits and regular contacts with constituents are fairly obvious strategies, but the web-based journal is unique in my experience.

Developing and Maintaining a Written Legacy

People in leadership positions commonly develop newsletters or similar vehicles for keeping their constituents informed. My purpose in developing a web-based journal, however, went beyond the mere sharing of information. I wanted a journal that could be truly interactive without becoming burdensome. Thus, the web-based journal *All Things Academic (ATA)* was conceived and has been published on the UA Provost Office and University Libraries website (http://libinfo.uark.edu/ata/) four times annually since 2000. I have used *ATA* to discuss positions, policies, and possible academic initiatives at the university through articles I prepare—at least one per issue. Some articles are coauthored with other leaders in the university (e.g., the chancellor, the dean of libraries). Recent titles have included "Arkansas Included—The Roles and Benefits of Research Universities,"

"Weathering hikes—challenging unreasonable library acquisition costs and maximizing benefits to the university community," "The Integrated Scholar—Have you seen one lately?" and "A Mosaic—Diversity at The University of Arkansas." Typically the feedback from these and similar articles is positive, the most common being comments such as, "What an effective way for our community to know what you are thinking."

Besides the articles, *ATA* contains two regular features: "Chronolog" and "Our Turn." "Chronolog" is an archive of congratulatory messages and responses between the provost and UA faculty, students, and staff. Each "Chronolog" contains three months' worth of messages.

If the individual congratulatory messages (to faculty members, students, or staff) elicit interesting responses, authors of the latter are asked if they approve of the publication of their responses. The feature is widely read, according to feedback I have received from constituents across the University.

The "Our Turn" section derives from communication vehicles I developed at the University of Connecticut and Washington State University where I served in chief research officer and graduate dean roles. The idea for "Our Turn" is this: Think of thoughtful notes and letters received by people in leadership positions and the time and energy the recipients put into crafting reasoned responses. So often just two or three people have opportunities to read the set of communiqués. What a shame. "Our Turn" provides the chance to share thoughtful communication with a much wider audience—of course with the permission of the correspondent.

The "Our Turn" feature has been popular, and I have used it to encourage myriad constituents to espouse their views. For example, it is not uncommon for a faculty or staff member to come up to me at a reception to share an idea or express a concern about the university. Often my response goes something like: "You make an interesting point. If you would like to share your thoughts with others and are willing to develop a thoughtfully conceived piece, I will consider publishing a work in the "Our Turn" feature of *All Things Academic*." Alternative but parallel scenarios involve occasions when colleagues write to me with a concern, and I typically respond, "You raise some very interesting points in your letter. Would you care to rework it for publication in "Our Turn"? As with "Chronolog," I have received some very positive feedback on "Our Turn." Most importantly, both features empower and encourage participation of colleagues within the institution.

Conducting Forums

Articles and the other features of a journal such as *ATA* can also be used in developing another communication strategy noted above. Specifically, thoughtfully developed papers and commentary on policies, initiatives, and new directions for your unit can become the bases of forums for discussion.

During my positions at the University of Connecticut and the University of Arkansas, I have used such published papers as bases for what I referred to as "Research and Graduate Education Community Forums" and "Academic Community Forums." Here's how they work: Following the publication of an article or other piece, all unit employees and the colleagues they serve are invited to an open forum. At the forum, I take ten minutes (no more) reviewing the issue described in the article—sometimes using a PowerPoint presentation. Copies of an outline or the article may also be passed out. The short presentation is then followed by a question-and-answer and discussion session (i.e., fifty to sixty minutes), which is usually lively and informative. The forums signal to your constituents that you care about their views, particularly on potentially controversial matters.

The modus operandi in thoughtfully preparing for your interview, following-up, and then developing the promise of a new position paper that indicates your intended actions and communication style—followed by a robust communication strategy and set of actions—represents a powerful start to a new position. The start is reinforced and sustained by effective communications with your supervisor—a topic we will consider in the next chapter.

Communicating with Your Supervisor

Leaders don't really run organizations . . . Rather, leaders lead individual followers, who collectively give motion and substance to the organization of which the leader is the head.

—STEVEN B. SAMPLE (1940–), president, University of Southern California

The idea of communicating with one's supervisor may seem obvious but is often lost on professionals. Of course, communication begins with listening but is amplified through meaningful dialogue, a commitment to regular interaction, and an understanding of the development of interpersonal strategies that work best among different pairs of individuals. Let's consider these points further.

Beginning with Listening Skills

In his book *Contrarian Leadership,* Sample (2002) addresses the topic of "artful listening," listening that leads to meaningful understanding. The listening strategies that support artful listening include the use of "I" and "we" messages that obviate defeating "you" messages. I'm sure you can remember a relative, teacher, or errant supervisor who was prone to accusatory "you" messages and how hurtful they seemed.

Artful listening also benefits from thoughtful feedback in which you frame statements such as, "If I understand you correctly, you are saying . . ." Another strategy involves questioning along the lines of "Could you state your position in another way?" An additional strategy includes a summing-up approach, wherein you say something such as, "I believe that we have come to an understanding that . . ."

Your use of artful listening may not be reciprocated by your supervisor but can go a long way in developing meaningful dialogue. A special "presence" also helps.

Being Truly Present

A Truman scholar once admonished, "Listen, hear, and be truly present." The advice is effective in listening and in dialogue, but the "truly present" part has often struck me as having a double meaning; that is, not only is it important to practice artful listening when speaking with one's supervisor, it is also important to listen carefully to their speeches and other presentations. In actuality, these efforts are often reinforced by supervisors' requests to review drafts of presentations, campus letters, and opinion/editorial pieces. Don't pass up the opportunity to read these works and make comments. Indeed, it has been my practice to share references, quotes, and anecdotes with supervisors, who have often incorporated such "value-added materials" in their writings.

Besides attending formal presentations or their equivalents, you should establish a regular pattern of interactions with your supervisor and direct reports. In my current post as provost, I set up monthly or bimonthly meetings with my direct reports, but I am available more or less 24/7 through e-mail.

My pattern of interactions with direct reports may not be ideal and indeed, I have worked for supervisors who had widely different preferences for interactions. Let's consider interaction strategies a bit more.

Interpersonal Interactions

I once reported to a provost who abhorred one-on-one meetings, and I found—after some bitter experiences—that the best way of interacting with this individual involved trying to second guess what was important to him, determining preferable or alternative courses of action to problems or initiatives, and then seeking opportunities for ad hoc meetings with him wherein I would describe pertinent situations in no more than a minute for each and seek approval for my recommendations. The arrangement may sound strange, but it worked satisfactorily.

Most supervisors I have reported to were not quite as eccentric as the one alluded to above, but even with regularly scheduled meetings and other arrangements about communications, I have found some aids to interaction that are most appreciated when I meet with direct reports. One involves written agendas for meetings—even the one-on-one variety. The delineated points help keep the conversations on track and assist with a second aid: avoiding having meetings go beyond an hour. Another aid to interpersonal interactions is timely follow-up. Actions agreed to during meetings are even more appreciated when a follow-up comes soon after the meeting. Thus, messages e-mailed to direct reports, with copies to your supervisor, will reinforce the effectiveness of meetings.

To sum up this chapter, communications with supervisors are facilitated through artful listening, commitments to regular interactions, and the crafting of interpersonal strategies that work best among different pairs of individuals. With agreements in place between supervisor and direct report, a new administrator will also benefit from "getting around" his or her unit. We'll consider this topic in the third and final chapter of this section.

CHAPTER

3

Getting Around

"Solvitur ambulando" St. Jerome was fond of saying. "To solve a problem, walk around."

—GREGORY MCNAMEE (1957–), American writer,
journalist, editor, translator, and photographer

We may never know if William Hewlett and David Packard were influenced by the sage advice of Saint Jerome, but their management technique, referred to as "management by walking around" (MBWA) became a concept adopted worldwide and one that is still practiced sixty years after its first use in the then fledgling firm of Hewlett-Packard (HP, 2005). According to the HP website, the MBWA technique was part of a management platform based on "personal involvement, good listening skills and the recognition that 'everyone in an organization wants to do a good job.'" Not a bad philosophy for any enterprise, including higher education, as we have already considered in the first two chapters.

While the MBWA technique, as conceived of originally, had somewhat of a "random feel" to it, I believe that the concept of "getting around" can have a powerful impact on an academic unit or community whether your role be chair, dean, vice-provost, provost, or other academic administrator. In the paragraphs below, I offer some strategies for getting around—strategies that have worked effectively for me at a number of institutions.

13

Defining Your Targets

Recently, a university faculty-development center director and department chair (Mallard, 1999), noted how she uses MBWA to drop in on faculty in their offices, arrange visits to class sessions, and develop relationships with departments and units across campus. She also espouses the MBWA method as one that may help build trust among colleagues as well as improve efficiency and understanding and a sense among the faculty of a chair's accountability for departmental operations.

As one moves from department chair to dean to central administrative officer, the territory for getting around in is larger, and it is wise for more broadly based administrators to partner with direct reports, before wandering around. I have known many effective decanal colleagues who schedule visits to departmental meetings—not all meetings but perhaps as many as one or two per year depending on the size of the college or school. The visits tend to prompt other invitations for visits to alumni or student events, and deans are well served in their responsibilities by accepting many such invitations.

For new deans, individual visits with faculty members represent an excellent strategy for getting started. I know of one dean who effectively used this strategy in a professional school with over ninety faculty members.

For chief academic officers, it is again wise to identify units or individuals for visits by soliciting suggestions from direct reports. New chief academic officers especially want to get out to visit with college or school executive councils or committees—typically composed of department and other unit chairs, heads, and directors. I also believe that visits to college or school faculty meetings are important, as are the meetings in individual departmental units. For chief academic officers at larger universities, it may take years to make the rounds to all units, but the efforts are highly worthwhile and represent excellent communication activities beyond the academic community forums noted in chapter 1.

Besides unit visits, I have, both as a vice-provost at two institutions and now provost, organized visits to prominent individual faculty members. For chief academic officers, such visits are enriched if they are scheduled with a vice-provost. I have participated in such visits both as a vice-provost for research accompanying a chief academic officer on faculty visits as well as a provost joining the vice-provost for research for individual faculty visits at the University of Arkansas. Conversations are facilitated when two academic officers are present, and the inevitable questions about resources for teaching, scholarship, and research are more readily addressed through the involvement of the institution's chief research officer.

Last, but by no means least, academic administrators should have regular meetings with students and student groups. I am a great proponent of meeting regularly with student governance leaders—undergraduate and graduate alike. Deans in particular should have advisory groups of students who offer feedback on college or school conditions and serve as sounding boards for newly proposed policies and procedures. As with all student groups, food is a draw, so if you are able to organize meetings around meals—pizza or other refreshments—all the better.

Now, you have scheduled a whole semester's meetings, perhaps with executive, college, or school faculty groups; prominent individual faculty members; and groups of students. What might you do during these sessions? Let's consider this question next.

What to Say and What to Do

Taking the wisdom of Hewlett and Packard to heart, you should use meetings of the type referred to in this chapter largely for listening—to the faculty, staff, and students you serve. But, there can be some useful structure incorporated into the sessions. For example, in meetings with college or school units or at general faculty meetings, it will be expected that you make some opening statements about the college or school (as dean) or the university (as chief academic officer, vice-president or vice-chancellor, or vice-provost). Why not start with some brief remarks about the state of the unit you represent and where you think it is going? Comment on strategic plans or planning processes. Offer some anecdotes and examples of equivalent academic progress you have witnessed or observed among faculty, students, and staff. But, be sure not to take too much time. Remember the prime importance of your being at the meeting is to listen.

As a prelude to meetings with units, you will probably want to telephone or have an assistant call the unit head to indicate your preferences for the content of the getting around meeting. Suggest that you are amenable to making opening comments, but you hope the unit head will make a short presentation on the strategic plan for the unit, highlighting aspirations and concerns. At the actual meeting and following the unit head's presentation, suggest that the meeting be opened for free-ranging questions and discussion. During the latter sessions, I purposely solicit comments and questions on any topic that may be on the attendees' minds. You might think that such an approach invites contentiousness, but in my experience the response to openness, on balance, is positive and welcome.

Now, what about individual meetings with prominent faculty? Here, the call ahead is crucial. I have known faculty members to become quite anxious when informed that the chief research officer or provost is coming to visit them personally. The typical thought—so I have been told—is "What have I done now!" So, make sure appropriate calls are made ahead of time to assuage any nervousness.

Interpersonal Interactions

During individual meetings, try to be as informal as possible. The casual conversation may drift in a number of directions, but I like to come away from such meetings understanding the faculty persons' scholarly and teaching interests, the challenges they face in doing their jobs well, and their aspirations. You'll conclude such meetings refreshed and encouraged because you will undoubtedly hear things like, "The provost has never come to see me" or "I am so appreciative for your visit." And, of course, you will benefit more than the persons visited.

For meetings with student groups, again the atmosphere and approach should be casual. Organizing meetings around meals or refreshments will help. Additionally, you will want to emphasize that you are there principally to listen to students' perspectives, challenges, and concerns. The expressions of support from the students will be positive particularly when they learn that you really care about their views on the policies and practices of the university or your academic unit.

Getting around takes us a long way toward our goals of serving and inspiring faculty, staff, and students. But, there is much more that can be done to serve the role of providing inspiration and direction, as we shall see in section II—next.

SECTION II

Offering Inspiration and Direction

PREAMBLE

Administrative responsibilities, particularly at the levels of dean or director and above, call for attention to academic community inspiration and direction. While you may lead by example (e.g., getting around visits), it is also good for your direct reports and the people they are responsible for to know what you are thinking and what you value. Thus, a medium for written communication (e.g., newsletter, on-line journal) and a pledge to oral presentations—planned (i.e., as noted in chapter 3) and otherwise—go a long way in developing an informed set of constituencies. Why not start with pieces on what it means to stand where you sit and how you came to serve in your present post? But don't stop there. Plan a series of papers that describe your administrative philosophies and values. Continue with pieces on the aspirations and challenges you hope to work on—collectively with faculty, students and staff—as a result of university-wide planning, which is typically led by the institution's chief executive officer. Be sure to include, as well, articles on initiatives that may help the institution take advantage of special opportunities (e.g., gifted and talented and honors programs) or face particular challenges (e.g., inclement weather, storm damage, and human tragedies). The types of papers, approaches, philosophies, and values noted above are found in a set of papers in this section. So, let's get started with "Where you stand is where you sit."

Where You Stand Is
Where You Sit

Journeys are the midwives of thought. Few places are more conducive to internal conversations than moving planes, ships or trains. There is an almost quaint correlation between what is before our eyes and the thoughts we are able to have in our heads: large thoughts at times requiring large views, and new thoughts, new places. Introspective reflections that might otherwise be liable to stall are helped along by the flow of the landscape.

—ALAIN DE BOTTON (1969–), Swiss-born English author

The aphorism, "Where you stand is where you sit," rings true across many sectors of society. In higher education, it suggests that your position in an institution helps shape your views—be they related to program development, philosophic perspective, or policy. The age-old advice rings true, but lately I have been suggesting an expanded expression of the stand/sit wisdom—especially to audiences composed of students and faculty members. The message to academic audiences is this: "Where you stand is influenced not only by where you sit, but also by where you have been, what you have said, and what you have written." The purpose of this chapter is to address this expanded message and suggest how it may be helpful to academic administrators of all stripes.

Views of the Landscape

No doubt you have attended university-based meetings in which participants preface their remarks with phrases such as, "Well, in our department we . . ." or "In our organization we . . ." The phrases are typically followed by perspectives that are narrow and often of limited value.

Professionals can broaden their views through contact with colleagues from a wide variety of disciplines within the institution. Thus, you may observe broadened perspectives among active members of faculty governance bodies and other significant university-wide service committees.

The take-home message is that one's perspective can be improved either through service in broadly responsible academic or administrative positions or faculty governance. Through such responsibilities or service, individuals broaden their capacities to serve their universities. But, one's "seat" in an institution is only one factor that influences the breadth of perspective. Indeed, places "where you have been"—particularly with respect to international scholarship and service—offer valuable perspectives for all members of the academy.

The Cosmopolitan View

If you have had like experiences, you are fond of suggesting to students that meaningful study-abroad experiences change their lives—forever. Those who doubt this view need only speak with students who have received some of the most prestigious fellowships and scholarships, such as the Rhodes, Marshall, Truman, and Goldwater awards. For example, it was not surprising in 2001 to learn that UA student, Anna Terry had won a Rhodes scholarship, given her prior study-abroad experiences in Europe. Similarly, the competitive position of UA student Michael Berumen for a Goldwater Fellowship and a three-year National Science Foundation (NSF) graduate fellowship was influenced in no small measure by his years at James Cook University in Australia as an undergraduate and beginning graduate student.

Besides their positive effects on students, internationally based scholarship and research have powerful effects on the perspectives of faculty members and staff. I have witnessed their results in economic development and education partnerships I helped craft or assisted in at the University of Arkansas, the University of Connecticut, the University of Texas at Austin, and Washington State University, as well as at institutions in Australia, Chile, China, Croatia, England, France, Germany, India, Italy, Kenya, New Zealand, Romania, Russia, South Africa, Thailand, Tunisia, and Venezuela. The development and nurturing of such partnerships will be discussed more thoroughly in chapters 24 and 25.

Besides international education, research, and scholarship experiences, professional speaking and writing efforts help shape perspectives.

What You Say and What You Write

Victorian essayist and philosopher, John Stuart Mill (1891) noted, "Hardly any original thoughts on mental or social subjects ever make their way among mankind, or assume their proper importance in the minds even of their inventors, until aptly selected words and phrases have, as it were, nailed them down and held them fast." Thus, the organization and description of one's professional experiences through oral and written reports are valuable adjuncts to broad-based experiences. Accordingly, one needs to take seriously the crafting of sabbatical or equivalent proposals—as well as reports that are filed after such assignments. It should be our hope as academic administrators that faculty members will convert their international education, research, and scholarship experiences into papers for oral presentations and publications in professional journals. Many fields (e.g., chemistry, education, engineering, mathematics, and nursing) have education journals that serve as good outlets for these kinds of professional papers. If such outlets are unavailable in particular disciplines, I encourage UA faculty to consider possible publication in the university's quarterly journal, *All Things Academic.*

In a work particularly pertinent to this section and the one immediately above on travel, Alain de Botton (2001) describes the powerful effects international travel and scholarship had on the creative work of artists and scholars from Charles Baudelaire to Gustave Flaubert to Edward Hopper to John Ruskin. We are all familiar with Herman Melville and Joseph Conrad and the seminal effects their sea travels had on the authoring of *Moby Dick* and *Lord Jim,* among many other works. Other examples of the impact of international research and scholarship include the German scientist Alexander von Humboldt (de Botton 2001), who, following a five-year study on the continent, reshaped the way the world thought about the natural science of South America. And, who can forget Albert Schweitzer, whose experiences in Africa helped shaped great works from philosophy to medicine.

In summary, you may wish to consider sharing your views on how teaching, scholarship, and service—broadly defined—may make a difference in academic perspectives. This consideration may be tied to a description of how your own experience led to the position you now hold. We'll consider an example next relative to the post of provost at a research university.

How Does One Happen to Become a Provost?

There are only two or three human stories, and they go on repeating
themselves as fiercely as if they had never happened before.
—WILLA CATHER (1873–1947), American novelist

P eople are intrigued and motivated by stories. Having a "short story"
of your professional career is useful whether you have to introduce
yourself to a group of alumni, students, or staff or if you wish to
imbed engaging anecdotes in presentations.

As you think about organizing your story, why not add some detail
and prepare a work that can be published as what might be called a story
article. During the crafting of your story, think especially about teachers
and other professionals who may have had powerful influences on your
career and successes and incorporate some relevant anecdotes and references. For example, a message of "here is what I wish for you" will not be
lost on your audiences.

As an example of a story article, I offer this chapter with a short ver-
sion of the Bob Smith story. The chapter is developed from a piece that
was crafted and published in *All Things Academic* in 2003. The story begins
with reference to a conversation with a colleague who posed the question
"How does one happen to become a provost?" My answer: "Well, it doesn't

just happen." But the juxtaposition of time, place, and events does influence opportunities. Indeed, the latter description fits the definition of what philosophers refer to as a "phenomenon," and for me, the phenomenon started as an undergraduate student at St. John's University in New York (SJU) and continued during graduate work at the University of Michigan (UM). I hope, through this short story, to describe how the SJU/UM phenomenon and subsequent opportunities in higher education assisted me in serving the University of Arkansas, one of America's leading public research universities, as provost and vice-chancellor for academic affairs.

Provosts are variously defined as high university officials, stewards of cathedrals or manors (references that date from medieval times), city officials (e.g., the lord provosts or mayoral officials in Edinburgh and Glasgow), or directors of prisons. While at times the job feels like all four, in higher education, it amounts to a post as chief academic officer with broad responsibilities for academic oversight across an institution—usually one with many thousands of students. Additionally, provosts are typically second-in-command. But, we need to return to the original question of how one achieves such a position.

My academic career began as an undergraduate at SJU. Having worked summers and weekends in community and hospital pharmacies during high school and college, I came to understand the level of practice my entry-level pharmacy degree would permit. Quite frankly, I perceived a level of practice that cried out for enhancement, so I began thinking of a career as a pharmacy professor, which might afford opportunities to influence changes in the profession. This aspiration led to a review of suitable graduate programs that would also support my emerging scholarly interest in pharmaceutical and medicinal chemistry. The support and encouragement of such ambitions was clearly manifest among the student-centered faculty and staff at SJU, particularly faculty members in the College of Pharmacy. For example, there were several faculty members who infused their lectures and laboratories with a passion for learning. Included among these dedicated souls was a dean (Andrew Bartilucci), who would someday become provost himself—of his beloved SJU.

There was also a very special associate dean—Hugh Luongo—who made all the difference in the world. Besides teaching freshman chemistry and attending to his administrative responsibilities, Professor Luongo would single out promising junior-level students for special counseling. I remember being called into Professor Luongo's office in the spring of 1962. After discussing prospects for graduate study, I heard him say, "Bob you are one of our stars. Someday, I hope you will have my job." It's a compliment I have always remembered and one that has served as inspiration throughout my career in academia. It is also a comment I have offered to many promising undergraduate students that I have counseled, hoping that it would be as inspirational to them as it was to me.

My experiences with SJU pharmacy faculty members was augmented by special mentoring from then assistant professor of organic chemistry, Eugene Kupchik, who would share a copy of *Selective Toxicity* (1960), along with this sage advice: "Read this book over the summer and we'll talk during the fall of your senior year about how you might nurture your interest in pharmaceutical and medicinal chemistry through graduate study."

Fortunately for me, the University of Michigan was highly recommended by Professor Kupchik and several of my pharmacy instructors. As a bonus, UM professor Joseph Sinsheimer (1922–1997) offered me a fellowship for my first year of study. More important than the fellowship, however, was the chance to work with Professor Sinsheimer. His love of students in general and his deep commitment to the mentoring of graduate students—each and every one of them—was critical to my development. One example turned out to be a choice of dissertation topics.

After working on Professor Sinsheimer's project funded by a National Institutes of Health (NIH) grant (i.e., isolation and characterization of antisweet components of the Indian milkweed, *Gymnema sylvestre*) during my first year, I approached him about possibly changing research areas. My reading at that time and a question on a comprehensive examination had stimulated an interest in drug metabolism. His response: "Sure. I have not been involved in such work but if you can come up with a good proposal for a dissertation project, I'll support your efforts."

A summer's work in the library led to a study of the comparative mammalian metabolism of the estrogenic hydrocarbon *trans*-stilbene and a new area of research—for both of us. For me, the work set the stage for a number of future research efforts. More importantly, the direct involvement in crafting the project and the freedom of exploration afforded by Professor Sinsheimer (also through—as I would learn subsequently—a NIH Training Grant) were as crucial to my development as the research itself.

Besides Joe—as he would later have me call him—there were other faculty and graduate students in the UM College of Pharmacy who were of great inspiration and support. Most notably, I include Ara Paul (especially his hands-on natural-products course), Joseph Burckhalter, Raymond Counsell, Bill Higuchi, and George Zografi along with fellow graduate students Larry Rampy, Subba Rao, Hugh McIlhenny, and Frank Sciavolino.

And, of course, all of this support took place in the intellectually and socially enriching university environment that collectively made my Michigan experience a touchstone for a lifetime.

With PhD in hand, I was ready to begin the academic career I had planned for. My first post was as an assistant professor of medicinal chemistry at the University of Iowa (UI) where I was promoted to associate professor and tenured in 1971. During my nearly seven years at UI, I taught undergraduate and graduate courses and pursued research in pharmaceutical analysis and drug metabolism. The research was supported initially through a coinvestigator relationship with my supervisor and mentor, Joseph Cannon, who was a professor of medicinal chemistry and principal investigator on a major NIH grant.

The collaboration continued for a few years but took an important turn three or four years into the effort when Professor Cannon came into my office one day and declared, "Bob, I have been delighted to work with you in this effort over the past few years, but it is now time for you to write your own NIH grant proposals and seek a 'principal investigator' position for yourself." I followed his advice and was successful the following year.

In the early 1970s, pharmacokinetics (i.e., studies of the absorption, distribution, metabolism, and elimination of drugs in animals and humans) was becoming of greater recognized importance, and I thought I should look for opportunities to broaden my perspective, using the foundations developed at Michigan and Iowa.

In 1973, I became aware of a new dean at the University of Texas at Austin (UT Austin), Jim Doluisio, who had founded a multidisciplinary research unit—the Drug Dynamics Institute (DDI). Fortunately, he had a faculty opening for an associate professor. I interviewed successfully and accepted the position with the proviso that I simultaneously be appointed as assistant director of the DDI. In three to four years' time, I would be promoted to professor and director of the DDI. In this latter role, I had the chance to further enlarge the scope of the institute to the point where we were pursuing a variety of studies from formulating creams and ointments for the National Football League to pharmacological studies of drugs with the potential to be abused to design and pharmacological testing of potential anticancer agents to socioeconomic studies in Latin America.

Besides the broad-based research of the DDI, my understanding of university research was further enlarged through service for eight years as chair of UT Austin's human-subjects review committee (i.e., Institution Review Board [IRB]). My service caused me to read more than one hundred protocols per year in fields as diverse as clinical pharmacy, education, kinesiology, music, psychology, and sociology. And, this service provided the inspiration to consider the next career jump from institute director to chief research officer at a major university.

The transition turned out to be more difficult than I had anticipated. After seeing my initial applications for chief research officer positions engender little or no interest, I discerned that it might be best to pursue an academic deanship as an intermediate position. This goal led to a move to the Pacific Northwest and acceptance of the deanship of the college of pharmacy at Washington State University (WSU).

I joined WSU in August of 1985 and was there only four months when I learned that Jack Nyman, vice-provost for research and dean of the graduate school, intended to retire in mid-1986. I remember hearing the news over the radio while driving from Pullman to Spokane on a snowy December morning and saying to myself, "Jack you can't do that. I would like to apply for your job, but I cannot leave this deanship so soon." So, a national search for Jack's replacement was mounted but failed to lead to a viable candidate during the remainder of the 1985–86 academic year. When the search was restarted in the fall of 1986, the WSU provost gave me permission to apply, and I got the job. One of the reasons that I was competitive was the scholarly work I had done in writing two books on research management while at UT Austin. Other assets included a broad understanding of university research gained through service assignments at three universities.

Now I had what I thought was my dream job. And, in many ways the combined post of chief research officer and graduate dean is one of the best in a university. Where else are you expected to learn about a myriad of fields? And, where else are you challenged with dealing with a variety of issues as broad as those arising in literally hundreds of programs?

I enjoyed my work at WSU, but in 1997 because of changes in top administrative officers, I felt that it was in my best interest to move on. After interviewing for positions from Kansas to Massachusetts, I was privileged to receive an offer of a post as vice-provost for research and graduate studies and dean of the graduate school at the University of Connecticut. Here, I had the privilege of working for Mark Emmert (who was provost and chancellor and who would later become chancellor at Louisiana State University and then president of the University of Washington) and learn about a range of programs and studies that significantly augmented my experiences at WSU.

Just as I noted in the discussion of the word "phenomenon," chance has a role in many of life's opportunities. On November 9, 1999, at 4:30 p.m. a call came totally out of the blue from Professor Greg Salamo, chair of the provost search committee at the University of Arkansas. I remember Greg's fateful question: "Do you think that you might have an interest in working at the University of Arkansas?" And, I remember my initial reply: "Well, I haven't thought about that today Greg, but let me share it with my wife and I will get back to you tomorrow." The subsequent interviews occurred in February and March of 2000, and I was on the job in June.

Serving as provost has been one of the most challenging yet satisfying positions in my life. And, the work has been facilitated by a congeniality and spirit of service encountered at the UA—comparable to that of no other institution where I have served previously. During my first six years of service at the UA, I was involved in a wide array of interesting developmental projects and efforts including

- Serving as executive secretary to the 2010 Commission (see also chapter 18), a ninety-plus-member group of state leaders who were charged by the chancellor to craft a ten-year plan that would ensure the positive impact of the university on the state's economic, cultural and intellectual life
- In connection with the 2010 plan, working with UA academic units to ensure pursuit of the UA's vision and academic mission, goals, and objectives, including benchmarking against fifty-three of the best public research universities in the nation
- Leading a team effort to review all of the university's doctoral programs at the behest of the Arkansas Department of Higher Education
- Working with the vice-chancellor for federal and community relations and the vice-provost for research to craft a federal government relations program to enhance funding to the UA
- Assisting in UA's commitments to diversify its faculty, students, and staff through an office of institutional diversity and education, the appointment of an associate vice-chancellor, and the mounting of several diversity initiatives;
- Publishing a quarterly online journal—*All Things Academic* (http://libinfo.uark.edu/ata/)
- Making more than eighty presentations per year inside and outside of the university

What's next career-wise? I'm not really sure. But perhaps I'll live long enough to offer an addendum someday. I do know, however, that my experiences at St. John's University and the University of Michigan—within and beyond my discipline, most especially in the arts and humanities—were critical to whatever success I have had in my professional life. These experiences were augmented throughout my career by the example and mentoring of many supervisors, several of which have become lifelong friends.

The influence of teachers—at all levels of one's professional life—is a powerful message of my story. In the next chapter, I will present examples of how the theme of teacher involvement can be developed further in written works.

CHAPTER 6

The Spirits of Our Teachers
Live in Our Souls

One looks back with appreciation to the brilliant teachers, but with
gratitude to those who touched our human feelings. The curriculum
is so much necessary raw material, but warmth is the vital element for
the growing plant and for the soul of the child.

—CARL JUNG (1875–1961), Swiss psychoanalyst

Ask any professional about the most influential persons in his or her
career and you will likely hear about a teacher or teachers. For
Edward R. Murrow, arguably the best broadcast journalist of the
twentieth century, it was Ida Louise Anderson, a diminutive and frail
Washington State University speech professor who inculcated in him a
love for words.

For Griffin Smith Jr. executive editor of the *Arkansas Democrat-Gazette*,
one of his most inspirational teachers was Charles Alan Wright, the
notable U.S. constitutional scholar at the University of Texas at Austin.
Indeed, Smith went so far as to change his name legally (i.e., to Smith
Griffin) for one year while he was in law school to improve his odds for
getting into one of Wright's courses. Apparently, because of the teacher's
popularity, students were enrolled in Wright's courses through a type of
lottery—based on the first letters of last names and the *S*'s were disallowed
the year of the Arkansan's quest.

For a third example, I consider it a near certainty that students of Christa McAuliffe, the nationally recognized teacher chosen to be an astronaut through a highly competitive selection process who died in the 1986 *Challenger* disaster, remember the influence of an instructor who claimed, "I touch the future, I teach."

There are clearly many other examples of teachers who have touched something fundamental in their students' lives or who have—as I like to think—populated the souls of former students. But, I would now like to offer some thoughts on the types of teachers we experience in our lives and how these different types of teachers serve as long-term sources of inspiration.

Teacher Types

Teachers may be thought of as one of three types: 1) instructor, 2) mentor, and 3) peer. These classifications will certainly overlap among teachers. But, individuals in the different categories have varying potential for impact on students—but none insignificantly. Let's take a little more descriptive look at each.

INSTRUCTOR

Everyone has experienced instructors as a type of teacher. Instructor-teachers tend to fit the model, which has rich historic roots, of the expert and authoritative teacher. Moses Maimonides, the great twelfth-century Talmudic scholar, wrote in his *Guide for the Perplexed*, "A man who has instructed another in any subject, and has improved his knowledge, may in like manner be regarded as the parent of the person taught, because he is the author of that knowledge." Thus, teachers who may only be involved marginally in students' lives may nevertheless be powerful influences particularly when the instructor-teachers are charismatic and gifted in their craft.

MENTOR

The concept of mentoring emanates from the great Homeric work, the *Odyssey*. Recall when Odysseus went off to the Trojan War—a journey that lasted twenty years (i.e., ten years for the war itself and ten years for adventures thereafter)—he left the responsibility for his son's, Telemachus's, personal and intellectual growth in the hands of his trusted friend Mentor. Thus, concern for and dedication to the holistic development of others has come to be known as mentoring. The mentor-teacher plays an extraordinarily important role in the intellectual, professional, and personal growth of students.

Anyone who has successfully completed a graduate degree, particularly at the doctoral level, understands the importance of great mentors. And, mentoring has taken on increasing importance in undergraduate programs, especially in cases of professional students with required internships and clerkships as well as for students engaged in scholarly and research projects such as those in honors programs.

Besides an interest in holistic student development, good mentors will serve as advocates and career advisors. Indeed, lifelong associations and friendships are common outcomes of the efforts of mentor-teachers.

PEER

Teachers may also be peers. Typically this happens when one conducts collaborative or interdisciplinary research. Particularly in the latter instance, teams of researchers are assembled with members having complementary skills and backgrounds. But, in the course of truly interdisciplinary research, new capabilities develop among team members because of synergistic interactions.

During my years as a graduate dean at two universities, I was fond of reminding faculty and graduate students that the best graduate programs are ones in which faculty-student relationships are quickly converted to peer collaborations. The resulting collaborations, in turn, provide great benefits to joint research efforts.

Teachers We Remember

If we polled any university's faculty members and students, I am confident that we would learn many stories about teachers who were notable instructors, mentors, or peers. For examples, I am able to share some personal experiences, as noted below.

INSTRUCTORS

The instructor-teacher examples come from experiences spanning a period from my undergraduate days to the spring of 2003.

Like many others, I recall vividly only a few lectures from my undergraduate days. But one lecturer and one presentation—in 1963, at that—stand out. The lecturer was Blaise Opulente (professor of English at St. John's University) and his message—to a group of pharmacy students—was this: "As an academic diagnostician I would like to prescribe three remedies as a possible corrective to the illnesses of excessive specialization, humanistic isolationism, an enfeebled emotional life, and spiritual starvation. These are 1) continuing education; 2) the reading of seminal books; and 3) the development of an interdisciplinary attitude toward science." I've had many occasions to return to Professor Opulente's prescriptions during my career in academia. For example, in chapter 16 the concept of Opulente's prescriptions is explored in the context of professional development of administrative support personnel.

Another instructor-teacher in my adult life is Barbara Harbach, who not only shared her insights on musical scholarship but also offered a powerful story and example of dedication in scholarship. Currently a professor of music at the University of Missouri at St. Louis, Harbach relates how—in the 1980s—she heard a lecture by a male music historian. During the talk, she was astounded to hear him say that, "If women composed anything, it wouldn't be very good and certainly wouldn't be performed today." That assertion sent Harbach off on a quest that has led to the founding of a scholarly journal (*Women of Note Quarterly;* http://www.vivacepress.com/) and numerous scholarly presentations that have helped illuminate the wonderful works of Hildegard Von Binham, Fanny Mendelssohn, and Clara Wieck Schumann, among many others.

My final example is a person whom I have not met but one who served as a great source of inspiration during the most recent U.S.–led war in Iraq. I am referring to National Public Radio reporter Anne Garrels, who reported every few days about the perils of a journalist caught in the thick of military action in the spring of 2003. Garrels offered not only views on the war from her room in a Baghdad hotel but also insights into the ingenious ways in which she protected herself from bodily harm, including working in her room in the nude so she could use the ploy of needing time to dress should Iraqi officials attempt intrusions at a time when she was making prohibited broadcasts.

MENTORS

In chapter 5, I shared the examples of Joseph Sinsheimer (University of Michigan) and Joseph Cannon (University of Iowa), who were my mentors in graduate school and during my first academic assignment respectively. I know of few better examples of mentors, and I was most fortunate to have experienced their fine efforts, from sage advice on teaching to gaining independence as a researcher to picking and choosing service responsibilities carefully.

PEERS

My examples of peer teachers come from experiences as a faculty member at the University of Iowa and the University of Texas at Austin. Jack Rosazza was a UI microbiologist and natural-products researcher whom I teamed up with in seventies and eighties to develop an area of research we dubbed "microbial models of mammalian metabolism." The purpose of this work was to discover microorganisms that could be used to produce valuable human metabolic derivatives of drugs and other chemicals that would otherwise be difficult to derive by other means.

Jack brought to the project superb understanding, skills, and capabilities in microbiology. I contributed knowledge and capabilities in analytical and pharmaceutical chemistry, which helped to advance the interdisciplinary work. In the course of the research, we learned a great deal from one another, and it turned out to be one of the most satisfying discovery-based efforts I have ever contributed to.

One of Jack's graduate students, Pat Davis, completed his PhD at the University of Iowa, and it was my good fortune to have attracted Pat to UT Austin as a postdoctoral student. In short order Pat became a peer collaborator in several successful projects. Today, Pat is an endowed professor and associate dean in the UT Austin College of Pharmacy.

There are many other peer-teachers I could cite from personal experiences. Some have been colleagues; others were supervisors or individuals who reported directly to me, but all contributed peer-teaching experiences that I have greatly valued. However, I know my experiences are clearly not unique, and I suggest that an article patterned after this one could be crafted and serve as an effective piece for many administrators to offer to their constituents.

Such an article might also serve as a segue into a series of articles on integrative scholars in one's department, college or school, or university. The concept of the integrative scholar and how a celebration of one's colleagues may serve as a source of inspiration and direction follows next.

CHAPTER 7

Promoting the Concept of the Integrated Scholar

There is no occupation so sweet as scholarship; scholarship is the means of making known to us, while still in this world, the infinity of matter, the immense grandeur of Nature, the heavens, the lands and the seas. Scholarship has taught us piety, moderation, greatness of heart; it snatches our souls from darkness and shows them all things, the high and the low, the first, the last and everything in between; scholarship furnishes us with the means of living well and happily; it teaches us how to spend our lives without discontent and without vexation.

—Cicero, (106–43 B.C.E.), Roman orator and
writer (as quoted in de Botton, 2000)

Scholars and scholarship are the lifeblood of colleges and universities. But, academic scholars in the beginning decades of twenty-first century have opportunities to blend research and scholarship (hereafter referred to simply as research) with teaching and service as no other generation has, in large measure because of what Friedman (2005) refers to as "the flattening of our earth"—technological assists to modern professionals and especially to members of the academy. The blending of research, teaching, and service may be thought of as integrated scholarship and adoption of this concept can be a great asset to modern higher education personnel—including administrators.

To assist in understanding of the integrated-scholar concept, I have in recent years instituted the practice of writing and disseminating a paper each year (Smith, 2002, 2003, 2004, 2005) to remind the academic community of the value we place on integrated scholarship—especially in tenure and promotion decisions. I also use these opportunities to highlight ten or more integrated scholars whom I have visited or otherwise identified during the past year or so through the communication strategies discussed in chapter 3. The purpose of this chapter is to describe the integrated-scholar concept and how it may be used to inspire and direct productive faculty efforts. The chapter ends with some tips on developing engaging biographical sketches of integrated faculty scholars.

The Integrated Scholar Model

In baseball, the triple threat is the player who can hit, run, and field—with aplomb. The faculty member who is outstanding in teaching, research, and service is potentially an academic triple threat. And, if an academician can create synergy among the three functions, she or he approaches becoming what may be thought of as an integrated scholar.

In my experience, faculty members generally understand expectations for teaching, research, and service from the moment they begin their career at a college or university. For example, in arts and sciences colleges it is not uncommon to encounter expectations, assignments, and performance evaluations for tenured and tenure-track faculty fitting a ratio such as 40:40:20—teaching, research, service. Furthermore, to achieve tenure and promotion to associate professor and then to full professor, excellence is typically expected in one or more areas. Such standards serve useful purposes—for self-guidance and for supervisors charged with evaluating performance. A drawback to the guidelines, however, is the implied notion that the three efforts are separate and unrelated to one another.

As suggested above—such a notion is not ideal. Rather, the mixing, melding, and indeed the integration of teaching, research, and service provides unique synergistic opportunities for excellence among faculty members. Bear with me while I elaborate a bit more.

Imagine a faculty member who consistently promotes active learning and infuses the fruits of his or her research into courses that he or she teaches. Imagine too—that same faculty member—publishing her or his teaching innovations in peer-reviewed journals and continually thinking about ways in which their scholarly presentations, creative performances, and professional development experiences may be incorporated into courses or other instruction offered to students. Additionally, imagine faculty members who plan and execute service commitments to complement teaching and research goals. Faculty members who envision their academic and extramural efforts as described in these musings are on the road to becoming integrated scholars.

In addition to incorporating the above ideas into published works (as noted earlier), I reinforce the concept of the integrated scholar in personal writings shared with faculty and fellow administrators. In all relevant publications, I offer advice to would-be integrated scholars.

Advice to Faculty Members on Integrated Scholarship

For the newly appointed faculty member or one who wishes to proverbially reinvent himself or herself, we might be asking, "What does it take to amass a record as an integrated faculty scholar?" Following is the type of advice I have offered to faculty members during the past several years:

- Maximize your teaching effectiveness. Sign up for workshops and other teaching-effectiveness seminars or programs offered through your university, perhaps through a teaching and faculty support center or equivalent unit.
- If you don't already—learn to love students!
- Determine how your instructional efforts, particularly innovations in teaching, might be written up and published. Many fields such as chemistry and communications have journals (e.g., *Journal of Chemical Education, Communication Education*) that provide excellent outlets for related scholarly efforts.
- Choose wisely your scholarly and research interests and foci. Pick areas, topics, and projects where you can make important contributions. Consider collaborations with well-established scholars and researchers. See how you might engage in interdisciplinary efforts that embrace your background and talents. Look for and apply for grants that may support your research and scholarly work, as well as undergraduate and graduate students whom you can engage in research. Use the services of your university's office of research and sponsored projects or its equivalent to assist in grant development efforts.
- Present papers at first-rate venues including meetings of well-recognized scholarly organizations.
- Publish articles in top-tier journals. If your area of scholarship (e.g., English, history) emphasizes the publication of original work in books—seek out the very best university or commercial

presses for publication. If your institution has a university press, see if the press staff members are willing to offer advice on publication outlets and opportunities.

■ Develop a plan for rendering service to your college or university, professional organizations, and society. In most tenure units, there are light expectations for university service at the assistant-professor level, but service expectations should not be nil. Choose college or university assignments wisely. Think about enlarging your commitments as you become tenured and anticipate promotion to full professor. After joining and participating in one or more professional organizations, think about seeking a place on organizational service committees or running for office. Consider service on editorial boards of noted journals.

■ Keep your chair and dean informed of notable accomplishments in teaching, research, and service.

■ Seek ways to integrate all of your university efforts. Ask for pointers from your chair and trusted colleagues. Place the topic of integrated scholarship on the agenda for a future departmental faculty meeting.

Advice—as sage as it might be—may not be sufficiently inspiring to faculty. However, I have found that publishing short biographical essays of faculty that you get to know through your academic administrative life will generate considerable interest in integrative scholarship and its fruits. Let's consider approaches to the essay development.

Writing about Integrated Scholars

The advice offered in chapter 3 ("Getting Around") suggested meeting with individual faculty. This is the best way to get to know faculty members who might be written up as integrated scholars. Other ways of gathering intelligence on integrated scholars can be sought through direct reports (e.g., deans or department chairs); that is, ask your direct reports to share congratulatory messages they write to notable faculty members in their units. You can also learn about potential integrated faculty members during regularly scheduled meetings with direct reports.

Once you have a list of candidates and information for a set of essays, you will need "hooks" to capture interest. Here are some hooks or introductory approaches that I have used effectively:

- If a measure of an integrated scholar's accomplishments is the success of her students, then _____ has hit the mark . . .
- He has only led his college's research center for three years, but in that time _____ has instituted teaching, research, and outreach programs that truly energize one another . . .
- Just as much at home in a laboratory, classroom, or a seminar for faculty, _____ is a prime example of an integrated scholar because of her . . .
- Known worldwide for his research, _____ is the quintessential opposite of the "ivory tower scientist" . . .
- Noted as a scholar who makes special efforts to engage under-graduates in path-breaking research, _____ exemplifies the best in integrated scholarship because of her . . .
- He has been at the university less than ten years, but _____ has made a significant impact through integrated scholarship in the field of . . .
- Students love _____ . . .

Once you have introduced and reinforced the concept of the integrated scholar in your academic unit or university, you may find—as I have—people using the term in meetings, in tenure and promotion packages, and in correspondence. This result can be very satisfying mostly because of its positive effect on faculty development. Similarly positive effects may accrue through the development and adoption of the concept of "intrapreneurial" faculty and staff, which we will consider in the next chapter.

Academic Intrapreneurs

Institutions such as government agencies, labor unions, churches, universities and schools, hospitals, community and charitable organizations, professional and trade associations, and the like need to be entrepreneurial and innovative fully as much as any business does. Indeed, they may need it more.

—PETER DRUCKER (1909–2005), Austrian-born
American management consultant and author

Reading the title of this chapter, you might be tempted to ask, "Academic what?" We are all aware of entrepreneurs—people who assume risk in new business ventures. An "intrapreneur," on the other hand, is one who works creatively within an institution to develop new associations and opportunities for advancing the institution's mission and goals. In the context of this chapter, the academic intrapreneur can be an administrator, faculty, or staff person concerned with finding new resources and development opportunities to address the fiscal challenges faced by many higher education institutions.

The purpose of this chapter—beyond giving life to the concept of the academic intrapreneur—is to offer a rationale for increasing resourcefulness in university enhancement and to review ideas and strategies for finding new sources of funding. Throughout, I will suggest roles that members of an academic community may play in potential intrapreneurial tasks.

Surveying the Academic Resource Landscape

Higher-education resources—particularly for public institutions—are tied to national and state economies. Accordingly, when economic conditions are poor, state support for higher education usually diminishes. This relationship is somewhat self-evident but is also complicated by priorities in state-government spending. In many states, higher education tends to be a fourth priority for legislators and other officials—trailing behind the funding for state prisons, Medicare and Medicaid, and K-12 education (i.e., not necessarily in that order), the last of which is often constitutionally protected.

In times of fiscal stress, one can imagine legislators, policymakers, and others thinking about funding priorities along the following lines: "We can't let people out of prisons," "We can't put people out of nursing homes" (particularly when state funding for Medicare comes with a substantial federal match), and "We cannot deprive our children of basic education." Thus, public higher-education funding is typically squeezed, especially when one considers that such institutions often have other sources of income, including tuition, fees (including fees for services such as resident dining and living), as well as extramural funding such as that provided through research grants and private gifts. Given such an overall picture, one can better understand how state funding for state universities and colleges in real dollars has decreased during the past decade, especially given the escalating demands for resources in areas such as criminal justice and health care.

When states' contributions to institutions' budgets decrease, there are the options of cutting back operations or finding other sources of revenue. Institutions often wind up doing both, but the pain of cutbacks is exacerbated by the fact that most higher-education institutional budgets are heavily laden with personnel costs (i.e., typically 60 percent or more overall but in many academic units, as much as 90 percent). Thus, budget cuts usually come with the prospect of lay-offs.

While reallocations and cuts in programs are likely to be continuing challenges in most higher-education institutions—particularly those in the public sector—academic intrapreneurs should be working creatively to identify and pursue options for new resources and opportunities for faculty, staff, and students. Let's consider some relevant ideas in the areas of extramural grants, public-private partnerships, and private development.

Extramural Funding

Sometimes people ask, "What is extramural funding?" For most academic administrators, the response will point to nongift funds that are attracted from outside the university, typically in the form of grants and contracts. The latter have so-called deliverables, which include research results, intellectual property (e.g., patents, copyrighted materials), reports, and services. Extramural grants and contracts also have negotiated indirect cost funds or overhead (or in federal parlance, facilities and administrative costs), which represents payment for basic infrastructural goods and services (e.g., purchasing, accounting, and physical-plant services) necessary for the successful conduct of research and other sponsored efforts. For further information and background on indirect costs—their calculation and negotiation of rates with the federal government see Kwiram (2004).

In 2004, the University of Arkansas instituted a salary-incentive plan tied to the successful pursuit of grants and contracts, particularly those obtained from the federal government, foundations, and private industry but not the State of Arkansas (i.e., to avoid the appearance of double-dipping). The plan pertains only to grants and contracts containing all relevant direct and indirect costs and provides personal financial benefits for faculty who successfully compete for grants that pay up to one-half of their nine- or twelve-month salaries (UA Academic Policy Series, 2004).

Specifically, faculty members qualifying for the incentive plan receive yearly lump-sum bonuses (i.e., up to 50 percent) from state funds freed up by salary paid through grants and contracts.

An obvious benefit to the incentive program includes potentially increased levels of research support with the attendant indirect cost benefits to the UA. However, there are less obvious benefits to this plan— benefits that go well beyond the particular investigators and directors of the relevant grants and contracts. Specifically, successful grantees help the UA free up vital state resources, which can be directed to the enhancement of teaching. Additionally, by having some faculty support their salaries, extramural funds are directed into salary adjustments thereby freeing up university funds, which can then be used for salary enhancements of non-grantee faculty and staff.

The take-home message of the proposed faculty salary incentive plan is this: While it is acknowledged that the incentive plan can only potentially benefit about one-third of a typical research-university faculty because of the nature of grants or contracts that will allow the budgeting of regular salaries, the dollars captured by the institution return very broad and significant benefits to the entire academic community. Additionally, a salary incentive program of the sort noted signals a type of activity that serves as a harbinger of other intraperneurial efforts, one of which includes public-private partnerships, which we'll consider next.

Public-Private Partnerships

During the past few decades, universities have entered into a variety of public-private partnerships to benefit teaching, research, and service programs. The efforts range from relatively modest residence inns that support baccalaureate hotel and restaurant or hospitality programs to high-technology business incubators to research parks that support significant economic development efforts. Frequently, the college or university provides land or facilities for lease. The private partners provide financial investment for the creation of a business or other nonuniversity effort. The benefits to these entities are obvious, while the college or university partner benefits from enhanced opportunities for research grants, student internships, and job opportunities for current and future students.

Are there other public-private partnerships that one might conceive of through an invigorated intrapreneurial mindset? Clearly, one can imagine other possibilities, perhaps in professional areas such as architecture or public relations. Might it be possible, for example, to attract private firms or perhaps non-governmental organizations to universities for infrastructure development and special training opportunities for students? Economists and public-policy makers are concerned about the export of offshore service jobs. Might university-based public-private partnerships offer possibilities for stemming the flow through cost-effective arrangements with apprentices who might gain special benefits from hands-on experiences? The possibilities deserve the creative thinking of faculty and staff across the academic community.

Yes, tax laws and conflict-of-interest policies have to be considered in crafting public-private partnerships. But, prospective arrangements can be scrutinized and aired publicly before initiation, and it is certainly worth the effort to explore the possibilities broadly.

One of the great advantages of public-private partnerships is that they offer the private partners the opportunities to learn much more about a college or university (see also chapter 24). And, such arrangements can lead to enhanced development and private gift giving, which we will consider next.

Development Efforts

Fund raising is big business at most colleges and universities, and the efforts are typically administered through a vice-chancellor or vice-president for advancement or an equivalent position. Activities are usually managed through a so-called centralized-decentralized model, which involves a central university development group (with the equivalent of a director who reports to the advancement vice-chancellor or vice-president) and a series of decentralized development offices and officers in all the major schools and colleges, and other units. The collective organizations are largely responsible for the phenomenal successes major universities have had in raising billions of dollars for everything from scholarships and fellowships to endowed faculty professorships and chairs to endowed program support to capital construction support.

Academic administrators who wish to inspire involvement by direct reports and faculty members in development work need to signal that development proposals are not the exclusive purview of a few. Rather, ideas for proposals come from a variety of faculty and staff intrapreneurs, and the ideas need to be vetted through the appropriate decentralized unit—typically at the college or school level. But intrapreneurs need to know that if they volunteer ideas, they should be ready to help contribute to the proposals knowing that benefits can accrue to their department or even to the intrapreneur personally.

As a younger pharmaceutical-sciences faculty member, I helped my dean (at UT Austin) develop an endowment that was used to create the James E. Bauerle Professorship that I was ultimately appointed to during the early eighties. The funds for the Bauerle Professorship came from a couple of pharmaceutical companies that the dean and I had worked with through grants to our university. The "ask" for nondesignated funds was built on several years of mutual trust and respect developed from successful completion of research projects.

Faculty members do not always feel comfortable asking for money. But with the help of development officers, preliminary ideas can be honed into effective proposals and participation in development efforts.

As faculty and staff intrapreneurs become more involved in development work, they usually become more cognizant of restrictions that frequently accompany private gifts. During the three fund-raising campaigns I have been involved in across as many universities, I have heard suggestions that the gift money raised be used for everything from faculty and staff salary increases to general tuition offsets to bailing out faltering programs. Unfortunately—and this is a message that needs to be proffered by academic administrators—gifts cannot be applied to just any need. Rather, gifts are typically made for specific purposes, and the purposes cannot be altered. Otherwise, the trust between institution and donor is violated. This is a hard message for some faculty and staff colleagues to swallow, but it is one that is commonly articulated in the world of philanthropy.

The most positive message for private development is this: Private gifts provide support for the margin of excellence among our faculty, students, and programs. The funds are rarely intended to supplant state or tuition support but rather provide support for extraordinary efforts that help convert a good institution into a great one. We will also consider development and fund raising—particularly in relation to planning—in chapter 18.

In summary, I hope that this chapter has illuminated the concept of the academic intrapreneur, enhanced understanding of sources of revenue, and offered some ideas for new intrapreneurs in the areas of extramural grants, public-private partnerships, and private development.

Just as an institution's financial strength derives from a diversity of resources, programs are enhanced when populated by diverse personnel who work in an environment that is comfortable and supportive. These latter topics are considered in the diversity chapter that follows.

Diversity—A Living Mosaic

I leave you love. I leave you hope. I leave you the challenge of developing confidence in one another. I leave you a thirst for education. I leave you respect for the use of power. I leave you faith. I leave you racial dignity. I leave you a desire to live harmoniously with your fellow man. I leave you finally, a responsibility to our young people.

—MARY MCLEOD BETHUNE (1875–1955), African American educator, from her last will and testament

People who travel the Mediterranean are likely to develop a heightened awareness of mosaics. These beautiful art objects, so prevalent in the ancient cultures of Athens, Rome, and Carthage—among others—suggest metaphors for the diversity we seek in all that we do in our academic communities. Through this chapter, I hope to further develop this concept and to offer some suggestions for initiating and promoting college- and university-wide diversity initiatives.

Look Carefully and Reflect

Mosaics—whether of ancient or recent origin—take on a different appearance depending on whether you observe them from near or from far. Up close, you note the individual pieces of different colors, types, and shapes. But, stepping back, the individual differences tend to recede, and new patterns and new levels of coherence are observed. But clearly, the strength and beauty come from individual differences—incorporated and blended effectively in diverse and artistically expressive ways. As will be noted more extensively below, the mosaic offers us metaphors for the characteristics of diversity sought in higher-education institutions, but first, let's consider a definition of the term.

Diversity may be thought of as a philosophic commitment to variety in people, places, and ideas—people of different genders, races, ethnicities, cultural backgrounds, beliefs, sexual orientations, abilities, and intellectual outlooks. Places that value diversity ensure a welcoming climate for different people and ideas—ideas that are developed creatively and expressed freely but always in a manner that respects the rights of other community members. Given this definition, we can explore how such a concept applies to the people, places, and ideas in the world of higher education.

PEOPLE

Individuals who speak about diversity, tend to begin with themselves—their gender, race, ethnicity, background, beliefs or worldviews, sexual orientation, disability, or some combination thereof. The logical extension is to move beyond oneself to colleagues in a department, school, or college. The more catholic thinkers among us—extend their perspectives to the greater university community, civic community, state, and nation. The most cosmopolitan among us will find it difficult to think of any community without considering a global or even universal context.

For our most cosmopolitan colleagues, thinking in a parochial or biased manner becomes counterintuitive and irrelevant. Consider, for example, the academic who has traveled and worked in different parts of the world—for illustrative purposes, let's just say, Asia, the Middle East, and Europe. Would an individual who has experienced the influence of myriad languages, literature, and religions, feel comfortable working among colleagues who act as though the world is made up of people of only one or two racial backgrounds and a single religion?

Even our less-traveled but well-educated colleagues begin to think in diverse terms following study, reflection, and scholarly work, particularly in the liberal arts. Thus, the biological and cultural diversity of the peoples of our world become not a threat but a reason to celebrate. The celebration is informed by the liberal arts, including the natural sciences, which confirm that racial differences are far less important than the biological and cultural commonalities of humanity. Study of the biological and social sciences also leads educated colleagues to the conclusion that any narrow definition of gender and sexual orientation is inconsistent with biological reality, which supports much greater diversity than a simple two-gender model (Fausto-Sterling, 2000).

While the sciences, particularly the biological sciences, help us sort through erroneous ideas about racial or sexual-orientation biases, the arts and humanities help us appreciate the vast array of backgrounds and experiences of our fellow humans. And, from study in the liberal arts—pursued in a welcoming and open environment—we come to understand the benefits of associations with diverse peoples. We also come to understand that diversity cannot be too narrowly defined or we miss the mosaic qualities that can grace and enhance our college and university communities.

Now that I have considered diversity relative to members of one's academic community, let me now turn to places or the environment that helps to nurture diverse people.

PLACES

A supportive climate must exist for an institution to become and continue to grow as a diverse community. And, only with such a supportive climate will the community benefit from the dedicated and creative work of its diverse members. Going back to the mosaic metaphor, climate parallels the mortar that holds the diverse pieces of mosaics together in beautiful and coherent patterns.

But, what may we say more specifically about institutional climate as it pertains to a college or university community? First, a favorable climate suggests that our colleagues and students are not uncomfortable being in a diverse community. Secondly, a positive and supportive climate affirms that we are continually looking for the content of character rather than appearance, as Abraham Lincoln and Martin Luther King Jr. admonished. And, when coupled with our constitutionally sanctioned principles of democratizing morality—life, liberty, and the pursuit of happiness—we have a powerful rationale for crafting the climate that supports diversity in our community. But as importantly, the strength, effectiveness, and aesthetic attractiveness of any college or university are ensured only insofar as we benefit from a variety of ideas emanating from a diverse community. Understanding this reality provides the third element of the diversity definition proposed above.

IDEAS

The gestalt of a mosaic is—most importantly—its effect on viewers. The gestalt of a diverse academic community includes the creativity and ideas that result when diverse people work in an environment that welcomes their creative work. Thus, while we may not agree with all that is said or all that is proposed by our colleagues, we recognize that it is important for these colleagues to have opportunities to speak out and for others to have opportunities to listen. Likewise, our community members should not be offended when their ideas are challenged or rejected because the merits of ideas are ultimately considered apart from those espousing them.

Beyond the respect we accord to the expression of diverse ideas, the well-developed diverse community understands how diversity ensures future creativity and richness of ideas. Again, going back to the mosaic metaphor, the beauty and strength of previously created mosaics—works of art and the human and institutional mosaics described herein—suggest that given diverse creative talent and excellent materials, additional works of beauty will be created. For the institution of higher education, a diverse community, combined with a welcoming climate, provides a fertile environment for a steady stream of new ideas and creativity.

So, how may we help develop and support a diverse academic community as an academic administrator? Let's consider this question in the context of some recent developments in colleges and universities nationally.

Setting Tone and Direction

Public commitments to diversity should come from top academic administrators, but these commitments must be reinforced by the conscious efforts of deans, department chairs and heads, and ultimately faculty, staff, and students. The mosaic metaphor or other models may be used to craft a vision for diversity at the institution and among its constituent groups. Examples of diversity statements among an array of U.S. institutions are available through the *Diversity Web* of the Association of American Colleges and Universities (2005).

With proclamations or statements in place, plans are needed for enhancing and sustaining a diverse community.

Looking across the United States, we find that practically every institution of higher education—at least in the public sector—is addressing diversity concerns and initiatives. The efforts usually begin with a highly diverse task force or campus-wide committee (i.e., typically appointed by the institution's chief executive officer) charged with addressing the following questions:

- What is the nature of the institution's diversity currently?
- How did the institution evolve into its current condition?
- What might be done institutionwide to improve and sustain a more diverse community?

Meaningfully addressing the "what" and "how" questions will not only lead to understandings of current "living mosaics" but also suggest directions for improvement and continuance. In my experience, the formulas for changes—coming out of the efforts of diversity task forces and committees—typically involve

- Leadership for diversity efforts
- Climate surveys
- Strategies and initiatives for recruitment and retention
- Climate initiatives relative to the workplace and learning environments

Let's consider each.

Leadership for Diversity Efforts

Few colleges or universities are positioned where they want to be relative to the diversity of their faculty, student, and staff groups. And, effecting positive changes not only requires proclamations but also leadership at the highest levels. The persons leading diversity efforts may report to different upper-level administrators in the organization from the chancellor or president down. And, in many instances, the leading diversity officer reports to the chief academic officer of the institution. However, in my most present post (i.e., University of Arkansas) an associate vice-chancellor for institutional diversity and education position was developed with the person filling it having dual reporting responsibilities to the provost and the vice-chancellor for student affairs.

Regardless of reporting responsibilities, the chief diversity officer should either come from a minority group or have a record of gender- or minority-studies scholarship. Of course, a combination of such a background and experience provide an ideal combination. Additionally, I believe that it is preferable to have a chief diversity officer who qualifies for a faculty appointment and tenure in a unit where diversity scholarship fits naturally. The tenured faculty status is important for the credibility that the diversity officer will need in discussions with other faculty members about diversity and its integration into the curriculum and related learning activities.

Besides high-level reporting responsibilities, a chief diversity officer should have a budget with some permanent discretionary funds to help start initiatives, typically in partnerships with colleges or schools and departments. The chief diversity officer should also play a major role in the development of other resources and their allocation as noted in a section below. Finally, the chief diversity officer should play prominent roles in the development, administration, and analysis of climate surveys that we'll consider next.

Climate Surveys

In all probability, few of us know academics that enjoy participating in surveys, but there are no better initial methods for assessing the diversity climate on a college or university campus. Indeed, surveys—well crafted to ensure and protect participant anonymity—represent one of the only ways of determining the presence of bias or discrimination within an institution.

Climate surveys should be developed through the efforts of the chief diversity officer working in collaboration with the institution's diversity task force or committee. The efforts will be aided immensely if the institution has a survey research center and the latter's service can be enlisted.

Separate climate surveys should be crafted for faculty, staff, and students, and the Institutional Review Board should review the survey proposals and survey instruments for human-subjects research protections. Examples of campus climate surveys can be accessed through the *Diversity Web* of the Association of American Colleges and Universities (2005).

A set of faculty, staff, and student climate surveys recently conducted at the University of Arkansas (Newman and O'Leary-Kelly, 2003) contain elements akin to surveys at other higher education institutions and include the following the inquiry areas:

- Participants' perceptions about the welcoming and developmentally supportive nature of their environments: departments or colleges, workplaces, and classrooms or equivalent learning spaces
- Participants' perceptions of personal safety in departments or colleges, workplaces, and classrooms or equivalent learning spaces
- Elaboration of supportive or prejudicial experiences of participants in departments or colleges, workplaces, and classrooms or equivalent learning spaces (e.g., helpfulness of colleagues and supervisors, discriminatory remarks by peers or supervisors, evidence of biased behavior, reports of threats to personal safety)
- Participants' beliefs and attitudes regarding departments or colleges, workplaces, and classrooms or equivalent learning spaces (e.g., level of satisfaction, apparent commitments of the institution to diversity and the principles of fairness, equity, and justice)

■ Participants' attachments to the institution (e.g., inclinations to leave or transfer to other institutions; feelings of being valued by colleagues, faculty, and staff; overall satisfaction with joining or coming to the institution)

Once the survey results have been collected and analyzed, a report can be prepared containing summaries of the results (i.e., prepared to protect the anonymity of participants) and analyses. The final report should be published on the institution's website and used by the chief diversity officer and other institutional officers to guide the development of initiatives for recruitment and retention of faculty, staff, and students. Let's consider this topic as the first of two useful outcomes of climate surveys and related reports.

Strategies and Initiatives for Recruitment and Retention

A good working principle for higher education institutions is for them to look like the people they serve. That is, the composition of the faculty, staff, and students should mirror the community served by the institution—be that defined by the state, region, or nation. As noted earlier, practically all U.S. institutions—at least those in the public sector—tend to embrace this mirror principle, and for many institutions its attainment represents a significant and often challenging goal.

To achieve a mirrored composition institutions have to consider recruitment and retention initiatives that will succeed in a competitive environment and in situations—in many fields or areas of study—where there are a limited number of underrepresented candidates to draw from as faculty members or professionals and prospective students. But, there are strategies and initiatives that have been used successfully, and many have been documented through newsletters and monographs. One chief diversity officer whom I respect greatly recommends works by Turner (2002) and Smith, Wolf, and Busenberg (1996). The *Diversity Web* of the Association of American Colleges and Universities (2005) contains references to a number of other useful works. Another work, resulting from the joint National Association of State University and Land-Grant Colleges–American Association of State Colleges and Universities Task Force on Diversity, *Now Is the Time* (2005), is also very useful. Additionally, Indiana University Purdue University Indianapolis (2005) has a website with links to recruiting initiative documents from institutions of varying sizes and types.

An even modest description of strategies and initiatives for the recruitment and retention of diverse faculty and other professionals and students would fill up this book, but there are some general ideas that are worthy of consideration. My list includes

- Recruitment partnerships with institutions whose histories include service to underrepresented populations of students (e.g., historically black colleges and universities or HBCUs)
- Strategic investment funds managed through chief academic officers' budgets but available for the hiring of underrepresented faculty and staff
- Mentoring programs for underrepresented faculty and staff that engage faculty and staff who are highly committed to social-justice causes or are themselves members of underrepresented groups
- Student scholarship programs that broadly define "underrepresentation" in socioeconomic, family higher-educational experiences, and regional terms as well as the traditional indices of gender, race, and ethnicities
- Student recruiters with multilingual and varied ethnic backgrounds or orientations who are given targeted assignments for recruitment of students from underrepresented populations

The above list offers just a few of the directions for strategies and initiatives. Work with chief diversity officers, diversity task forces or committees, deans, chairs and heads, faculty, and other professionals (e.g., admissions and financial aid officers) will lead to a wealth of additional ideas, strategies, and initiatives.

Diversity efforts take dedication and commitment at all levels of the institution and a willingness of all key players to accept responsibility and accountability for outcomes. But, success is measured not only in numbers of diverse faculty, staff, and students but also in the development of a nurturing environment. Let's consider this topic next.

Climate Initiatives Relative to the Workplace and Learning Environments

Armed with an understanding of the current diversity climate and commitments to strategies and initiatives to enhance diversity on campus, an institutional community should go forward with a shared understanding of vision and goals. The vision, as noted earlier, should embrace the philosophical notion that creativity and scholarship are not only informed by a diverse environment but also ensured of continued vibrancy through people with diverse backgrounds and ways of looking at the world. These values and perspectives need to be infused into all components of academic life, including the curriculum. But, the latter poses a challenge for academic administrators.

While higher-education administrators have much to say about the organizational and operational aspects of their organizations, they risk a loss of trust and respect if they direct the content of curricula. However, having the principles and examples of diversity infused in various ways throughout the curriculum should be a key goal of higher-education communities and administrators, and the latter can play a role in raising questions and offering suggestions for inclusionary efforts.

Curricular efforts, particularly as they relate to general education, are the purview of the faculty as articulated through faculty governance organizations such as faculty assemblies or senates. These bodies will typically have general education or curriculum committees with representation not only from the faculty but also from the office of the chief academic officer. If the institution's chief diversity officer is a tenured faculty member, why not seek his or her appointment to such committees. Parallel efforts can be pursued at college or departmental curriculum committee levels through the appointments of underrepresented faculty.

To support inclusionary curricular discussions and innovations, retreats and workshops can be organized to heighten awareness of the latest thinking on diversity and curriculum matters. The best thinking from these and related efforts can be organized as a set of resources available through a university website. Three of my favorites include websites at Indiana University Purdue University Indianapolis (2005), the University of North Carolina at Chapel Hill (2005), and the University of Wisconsin-Madison (2005). Information on these sites can be supplemented by materials assembled through the *Diversity Web* of the Association of American Colleges and Universities (2005) and by your university librarians who you might engage in a joint website project with the collegiate units and offices of the chief diversity and academic officers.

Developing and infusing diverse elements throughout the curriculum is a goal that may take years to accomplish, particularly since some faculty resistance can be encountered especially among senior faculty who may perceive the efforts as a fad or an outgrowth of political correctness. But, there should be improved prospects for success working with more recently hired faculty particularly if they have had welcoming and supportive experiences from their earliest days within the institution. Here is where academic administrators play a role.

Imagine an institution where diversity is noted as a priority from the first day of faculty orientation through many days thereafter. Imagine an institution where new faculty and staff are expected to attend uniquely crafted workshops on diversity. Imagine an institution where feedback on the quality of the university climate is continually assessed to ensure its welcoming and supportive nature for all members of the community. Sound Pollyannish? Well, that scenario exists in many institutions, including institutions in which I have served on the faculty and as a staff person. And, the scenario is one that merits consideration in all higher-education institutions in our pluralistic democracy, not only as a matter of social justice and equity but also as a matter of sustaining what should be one of our country's most cherished resources—higher education.

In summary, I have used the characteristics of mosaic art as a metaphor for diversity and its possible components in higher-education institutions. These components—people, places, and ideas—were further described in terms of their functions and interactions, particularly as they relate to institutional diversity efforts. The latter were delineated as roles for administrative leaders; climate surveys; strategies and initiatives for recruitment and retention of diverse faculty, staff and students; and fostering a welcoming and supportive environment. The take-home message throughout is that diversity is everyone's responsibility but primary responsibility and accountability fall on the shoulders of academic leadership from executive officers to deans to chairs and heads to support staff leaders.

Moving on in this section on offering inspiration and direction, I now offer two professional development chapters that are among my favorites, beginning with one on speaking and related communication skills.

Ties That Bind

Adding Drama and Intrigue to
Speeches and Other Presentations

The ties that bind
Now you can't break the ties that bind
—BRUCE SPRINGSTEEN (1949–),
American singer, composer, and guitarist

Picture this. You come out onto a stage to give a talk. The stage is empty but for a podium and an easel supporting an object draped by a cloth. Whether you refer immediately to the mysterious object or leave it covered throughout the presentation, the effect is the same: it changes the dynamics of the presentation by posing a question. The audience can't help but anticipating, and wanting, the answer. Surely you will unveil the object at some point. But what might it involve? How might it relate to the presentation? You can imagine such anticipatory thoughts in the minds of audience members.

My guess is that we have all been at award ceremonies where relatively standard plaques or framed awards remain cloaked until the awards are made—and we usually know what to expect. But this practice can be adapted to all kinds of presentations using objets d'art or other props to bring home a point and to inject the drama of the unexpected into a presentation.

The drama works. I have witnessed this tactic to unveil—at a speech's end—an unknown item, to make concluding points.

The novel use of objects is one many strategies for incorporating drama and intrigue into formal talks and other presentations. Others involve the novel use of geographical, historical, literary, and popular culture references and sartorial accessories, to name a few. But, I want to return to the use of art before moving on to some of the other elements.

Use of Objets d'Art and Other Objects as Props

To exemplify the effectiveness of objets d'art in speeches and other presentations, consider using a painting depicting the myth of Theseus and the Minotaur to illustrate "consilience"—a term coined by the Pulitzer prize–winning biologist Edward O. Wilson and explained in *Consilience* (1998). Consilience, or the unity of knowledge, is the concept that all fields or disciplines can be connected when crafting a unified understanding of our natural and cultural worlds. Wilson illustrates this point by alluding to the Greek myth of Theseus and the Minotaur.

Briefly, Theseus was engaged by King Minos to slay the half-bull–half-man Minotaur—a monster who was responsible for the deaths of countless Greek citizens. For Wilson, Theseus is humanity, the Minotaur a metaphor for human irrationality, and the Cretan labyrinth—the home of the Minotaur—the challenge we face in conquering irrationality by connecting cells (metaphors for disciplines or areas of study) in just the right pattern to achieve understanding. Of course, the story is incomplete without Ariadne, the amorous daughter of Minos and the weaver of the golden thread that allowed Theseus—the hero—to descend into and return from the labyrinth after slaying the Minotaur. Ariadne's thread, therefore, becomes the metaphor for consilience or the notion of connecting many fields of scholarship (or disciplines if you wish to make a point about interdisciplinary research of scholarship) to achieve holistic understanding.

I have used a variety of objects in a fashion that parallels the use of the painting of Theseus and the Minotaur above. For example, after presentations containing allusions to the Antoine St. Exupery's great book, *The Little Prince* (1943), I unveil a fifteen-inch Le Petit Prince doll seated on a miniature chair.

Beyond the experiences noted above, you might consider others' use of props to make dramatic and intriguing points. For example, Buzz Aldrin, one of the first Astronauts to walk on the moon (along with Neil

Armstrong in July of 1969), begins talks with the public display of a Buzz Lightyear doll (the character in the Disney film *Toy Story*). John White, National Science Board member, uses imaginary nanoparticles sprinkled on the face of a lit overhead projector to make the point about their sub-microscopic size. For a contrast in scale, who can forget President Reagan's address to Congress when he stood by a mountain of U.S. budget books and referred to the assemblage as a "behemoth"?

Nancy Talburt, detective-novel scholar, has suggested the use of Matryoshka (Russian nesting) dolls as a metaphor for the unveiling of truth in stories of intrigue and presentations thereof. This is a fascinating idea that she derived from the opening sequence of the television produc-tion of John Le Carré's *Tinker, Tailor, Soldier, Spy* (1974).

Several years ago, I participated in a joint effort of the University of Washington (UW) and Washington State University to convince the Wash-ington legislature of the wisdom of investing in an Advanced Technology Initiative. As a part of this initiative, Robert Miller of UW (in 2006, vice-chancellor for research at the University of California, Santa Cruz) and I made a series of presentations to the Washington State House and Senate Commerce and Labor Committee, Higher Education Committee, and Trade and Economic Development Committee on the features and pro-posed merits of the multimillion dollar proposal. We were attempting to make the case that modern university-based researchers are capable of not only doing good basic research but also assisting the start-up of high tech-nology companies, which could be of great economic benefit to the Evergreen State. For use during the joint presentations, we chose artifacts that exemplified the types of value-added products that result from research.

UW's artifact was a vial containing what appeared to be a sample of water. But, as Miller held the vial above his head, he noted to the state rep-resentatives and senators that the water-white liquid was actually a solution of a reagent discovered and developed by a researcher in the UW Medical School—a reagent highly valuable in the diagnosis of osteoporosis.

The artifact presented by WSU was a sample of what appeared to be angel-hair that one might find on a Christmas tree. However, the product was actually a siliceous material that was derived from basalt rock (abun-dant in eastern Washington) by a unique process discovered and developed by a WSU engineering professor. You can imagine the legislators' fasci-nated looks when samples of basalt rock and the angel-hair product were held up side-by-side. The fascination increased when I described the eco-nomic potential of the product as a fire-resistant and environmentally safe insulation of possible interest to the U.S. Navy.

The impact of the UW and WSU artifacts was further enhanced when we circulated them among the legislators for closer inspection. Miller and I recalled one legislator remarking, "How do people come up with things like this?" That is a reflection of true drama and intrigue.

Before moving from props to other approaches to adding drama and intrigue to talks, let me offer a couple of additional ideas that may seem unorthodox but work impressively.

When Nelson Rockefeller was governor of New York, he reportedly had a sizable desk in his office with a stepladder hidden behind what seemed to be a set of drawers. When the press corps came to see him, he would dramatically reach down, pull out the stepladder, and ceremoniously climb onto the top of his desk from where he could address his visitors and subsequently answer questions.

One can use permutations on the Rockefeller technique by standing on desktops or chairs prior to addressing groups. Of course, I always remove my shoes first lest I mar a desk surface or soil a chair cushion. The act of removing your shoes in and of itself is dramatic.

Another variation on this theme is to climb a six-to-eight-foot stepladder before making a short set of remarks. After so doing, you can refer— for interest—to the stepladder as one of only a few props that was used in the original Broadway production of Thornton Wilder's Pulitzer Prize–winning production of *Our Town* in 1938.

One time when I used the stepladder technique, I had a colleague come up to me afterwards to say, "I thought you had lost your mind when you brought out that stepladder." Another more admiring colleague confessed the thought, "Where's my ladder?"

Objets d'art and a variety of other props represent just two of a set of strategies that can be used to build drama and intrigue into speeches and other presentations. Additional strategies run the gamut from novel geographical and historical references to integrating allusions to literature, biography, and popular culture (including short performances) to sartorial accessories. Let's explore these strategies and objects a bit more.

Delving into the Humanities and Social Sciences for Novel References

Maps, flags, and other symbols and representations can be incorporated artfully into talks through audiovisual aids. In 1995, I gave a plenary talk at a sustaining agriculture conference in Cote d'Ivoire. The conference participants were mostly governmental agricultural officials from nations in sub-Saharan Africa. Thus, I had a special opportunity to craft linkages to audience members through art incorporated into the talk's slides, which were prepared before the common use of PowerPoint. Today, the task would be facilitated by artwork readily available through the World Wide Web (e.g., *World Factbook*, 2005).

In any case, on each slide for the talk, printed material was superimposed on individual outlines of the countries and flags of participants at the meeting. Thus, audience members could feel a special identification with the presentation material—beyond its substance. One drawback to this approach—of course—is that you may miss someone's country. But, a preliminary apology for possible omissions should suffice.

Historical references offer novel ways to begin presentations. I have found that such references—developed through links in time—appeal to audiences of varying educational backgrounds. For example, you can use historic events of the day to spark interest in particular portions of your presentation. This approach involves using an Internet source such as IdeaBank (2005) or the *New York Times* website (2005) to determine historically important events of the day of your talk and relating these events—in dramatic and intriguing ways—to the theme of the presentation. Following are just two examples of this approach—examples taken from welcoming remarks or comments made to groups about impending events.

> **PRESENTATION ONE:** A New Year's social event honoring the accomplishments of senior University of Connecticut academic staff.
> **Date and Historical Events:** January 9, which is the date that Connecticut become the fifth State to enter the Union (1788) and the date of the ancient Roman Agonium Festival—in honor of Janus, the god of beginnings, doorways, and archways
> **Remarks or Context**: Comments about the interesting coincidence of the evening's event with an important day in the history of the State of Connecticut; also, the Janus festival allusion was used to highlight past events and prospects for newly hired staff in the New Year
>
> **PRESENTATION TWO:** Faculty and staff retirement reception.
> **Date and Historical Events:** On the day of the presentation, May 17, important events occurred relative to the topics of separation, anxiety, and new beginnings. For separation, Norwegians honor their separation in 1814 from Denmark; for anxiety, inaugural use of the first merry-go-round set up at a fair in Turkey in 1620; for new beginnings, Abraham Lincoln nominated for the presidency in 1860
> **Remarks or Context:** These historic events tie into three key characteristics of retirement and the experiences of professionals who are retiring, namely separation, anxiety, and new beginnings.

Combined allusions to literature, biography, and popular culture offer a treasure trove of dramatic and intriguing material for presentations. For example, the *Wizard of Oz* (1900) provides a powerful set of allusions for talks to students and parents alike.

Practically everyone is familiar with the 1939 classic film *The Wizard of Oz* starring Judy Garland (Dorothy), Ray Bolger (the farmhand Hunk and the Scarecrow), Jack Haley (the farmhand Hickory and the Tin Woodsman), Bert Lahr (the farmhand Zeke and the Cowardly Lion),. Frank Morgan (Professor Marvel, the OZ gatekeeper, and the Wizard of Oz), Margaret Hamilton (the evil Kansas neighbor, Miss Gulch and the Wicked Witch of the West), and Billie Burke (Glinda the Good Witch of the North). However, you will find relatively few people who have read the original Oz book or any of the dozens of follow-up volumes that were written and published after L. Frank Baum's original 1900 work. In fact, if you haven't read the book you may be surprised to learn of one of the important differences between the film and the book; that is, while Dorothy's adventure was a dream in the film, in the book she really went to Oz. And, Oz took on geographical and cultural characteristics that became the platform for more than forty sequels that Baum and his successors wrote well into the second half of the twentieth century. Indeed, Baum wrote twelve sequels from 1900 to 1919 the year in which he died. Interestingly, the writer of the greatest number of Oz books was a woman, Ruth Plumy Thompson, the fact of which represents an interesting anecdote to share with audiences.

Some scholars believe that Dorothy represents the girl child that Baum never had. Thus, akin to Lewis Carroll, Baum wrote *The Wizard of Oz* for children near and dear to him; in Baum's case—his two sons and their young friends. But, like so many great tales written ostensibly for children, the Oz story has a message of great value for all professionals. Why? Because the Oz story embodies the theme of social leadership, which is centered about the values associated with the Scarecrow, the Tin Woodsman, and the Cowardly Lion, namely, intelligence, kindness, and courage. Perhaps in an earlier time we would have said faith, charity, and hope—in that order. This allusion and the background noted are well received by many audiences.

Additional allusions have been adopted from the music world. Song titles and lyrics—referred to properly and used sparingly under fair-use provisions of U.S. copyright law—prompt special recognition and provide intriguing approaches to analogies and symbolism in presentations. For example, the line, "Where have you gone Joe DiMaggio?" from the Paul

Simon and Art Garfunkel song, "Mrs. Robinson," has served as one-half of a hyphenated title to a research ethics talk that I have given before numerous academic groups. The title and a few other lines of the song—help to draw the audience into a talk that requires discussion of several dark elements of human behavior. For example, one can ask the audience to recall the song's lines "We'd like to know a little bit about you for our files," "We'd like to help you learn to help yourself ," and "Hiding in a hiding place where no one ever goes," which help to set the mood for some of the sober research ethics topics to follow.

You can also use the title and a few lines of a Jim Croce song to help craft talks used to welcome new faculty and staff at orientations and related social events. Following a poignant reminder to audiences of the untimely death of Croce at thirty-two (in an airplane accident in Natchitochcs, Louisiana, on September 20, 1973), you can point out one of his most famous songs: "Time in a Bottle." After which, you may begin reading the last few lines of the first two verses of this haunting song, which contain the following elements: 1) What if we could save time in a bottle? 2) If we could, we would like to spend eternity with the ones we love (verse 1), 3) There never seems to be enough time to be with our loved ones, and 4) Who are the ones we want to spend our lives with (verse 2)? The actual lyrics are very powerful in their effects on audiences.

You can also note that the time in a bottle metaphor may serve as an extension of a common childhood fantasy about putting a message in a bottle and casting it into the ocean with the hope that some unsuspecting beachcomber in a far-off land will find it, relish the shared thoughts, and contact the sender. One can note at this juncture in the presentation that two women—in their teens—did cast a message-bearing bottle into Long Island Sound in 1979. The bottle was subsequently retrieved along the Irish Coast in 2000!

After sharing the Croce lines and the note-in-a-bottle anecdote, the spoken message may be followed by allusions to the advice of Thoreau (1854), Buscaglia (1982), and many other sages—that life is not all goals and accomplishments but "getting there." For new employees, the gentle cajoling is that it is important to treasure moments with colleagues, students, and friends during one's years at the institution—to save as it were their time in a bottle—in order to savor these memories in the years ahead. This conclusion is received with appreciation and joy.

A final set of recommendations involves the use of sartorial accessories such scarves and neckties, thus the chapter title's reference to "ties that bind."

Finding Props in the Clothes Closet

If you're a man, you probably either love or hate neckties. I happen to love them and might even be a called a necktie collector. And, I love to wear them on occasions when I have to give a speech or otherwise address an audience. In these cases, the tie is chosen with a theme that accentuates the talk and the epilogue comment begins with, "Those who know me well, also know that I like to wear a necktie that embodies a theme integral to my overall presentation. Today I am wearing . . ."

Following are just a few examples of my sartorial references:

- Presentations to faculty groups on research and scholarship in the arts and sciences have included references to a necktie containing detail from a Tiffany dragonfly design. The combination of artistic and technical talents of Louis Comfort Tiffany help me make a point about these different sides of creativity, which are often necessary for outstanding scholarship in both the arts and sciences.

- My University of Arkansas necktie collection includes one with images of the Old Main tower and another with the university seal. I have used these neckties to punctuate many presentations to prospective students and their parents, to faculty and student assemblages, to retired faculty and staff, and to alumni groups. The tower tie is used to make the point that the towers of Old Main have been beacons of hope and pride for all Arkansans, beacons that have signaled—north and south, east and west—the academic strengths of the university.

- At memorial services I have worn a necktie depicting the great *fin de siècle* Scottish architect and artist Charles Rennie Mackintosh's Rose and Teardrop design, which represents the joy and pathos of life and the mixed feelings that inevitably permeate memorial events.

If you are a woman, you may feel left out of the necktie game. Don't despair. Female colleagues at Spelman College and the University of Texas Medical Branch at Galveston have adopted parallel practices—using scarves. A third female colleague at the University of Connecticut employs unique colors and patterns in suit jackets to illustrate epilogue points. A staff professional at the University of Arkansas has noted how she uses designs in dresses as reference points for comments during presentations.

So, whether you adopt the necktie game—or something analogous—you may wish to consider ties that bind for connecting with audiences in special ways.

The uses of sartorial adjuncts to presentations need not be limited by the examples noted thus far.

If you have given a fair number of talks, you have certainly experienced the situation in which you are asked to address a group that has crafted a T-shirt with the group's logo or representation of a particular professional event. If you are given one of these T-shirts as part of your introduction, by all means consider putting it on as a prelude to your presentation. Few gestures will help you bond better with an audience than this dramatic act.

There are additional sartorial accessories that can be used to enhance drama and intrigue in talks. Consider, for example lapel and other decorative pins and awareness ribbons.

Even before the horrific events of September 11, 2001 (the day that gave new meaning to the term "nine-one-one") in the United States, I wore lapel pins. Not just those of a patriotic variety—which have proliferated after 9/11—but also institutional pins and pins commemorating certain artistic or architecturally significant works or interesting logos.

I wear lapel pins not only on jacket lapels but also on turtleneck shirt collars, shirt pockets, and badges that are issued at professional meetings or events. Why? Primarily because they provide clues to messages that I wish to portray formally and informally, but especially during talks.

Most universities have seals, symbols, and logos that are often crafted into lapel pins. The resulting pins offer symbolism that can be transformed into effective points in talks. Following are descriptions of just two of my favorites:

■ The official seal of the University of Connecticut (and no doubt many other universities) contain oak garlands or other representations of oak trees. It is intriguing to point out to audiences that the oak, from the time of ancient Greece, has been a symbol of wisdom, strength, and longevity. What better characteristics are there to associate with institutions of higher learning? What better characteristics to weave into talks about the growth and development of people and institutions?

■ Flag pins became very popular in the United States following September 11. I also like to collect friendship pins with flags of two countries or a country and a state juxtaposed. Thus, I have pins with flag pairings such as the United States and Italy and the

United States and South Africa, which commemorate or remind me of university partnerships that I may wish to describe as a component of a presentation.

Since many audiences will include professionals who are affiliated with a variety of governmental, business, or professional organizations or have unique professional or social interests, you can undoubtedly think of seals, symbols, and logos that might have interesting characteristics for references in presentations.

Beyond lapel pins, you can imagine a host of other sartorial accessories from awareness ribbons to belts to caps to jackets to sweat shirts, all of which could depict interesting symbolism for references in talks. As I suggest to others—just let your imagination run wild.

Crafting and giving presentations can become a special component of life. Time spent crafting and giving presentations has special rewards—professionally and personally. For one, speechmaking helps you find a signature for your personality and professional creativity. In various places where I have worked, people call me the "tie man" because of my signature use of neckties to make points during talks. When I walk into a room where I am about to speak, and there are people present who know me, one or more will come up, look at my necktie and ask, "How is that necktie going to be woven into your remarks today?" My typical response is "You'll see." And so, the mystery, the drama, and the mystique grow in proportion to your reputation as a dramatic and intriguing speaker.

Speechmaking and other forms of communication are vital components of the professional lives of academic administrators. In the next chapter I'll offer some additional thoughts on the joys, challenges, and failures of professional life with particular reference to the word of academia.

Understanding the Joys, Challenges, and Failures of Academic Life

I perceived that you had acquired some knowledge . . . from others, and that you were perplexed and bewildered; yet you sought to find out a solution to your difficulty. I urged you to desist from this pursuit, and enjoined you to continue your studies systematically; for my object was that the truth should present itself in connected order, and that you should not hit upon it by mere chance.

—MOSES MAIMONIDES (1135–1204), Talmudic scholar, philosopher, physician and author of the broadly influential text The Guide for the Perplexed (1190)

Seemingly on cue from Maimonides, many of us have observed, studied, and sought a "connected" understanding of what it takes to be a successful professional—not in the twelfth, nineteenth, or even twentieth centuries, but now in the twenty-first century. In my case, earlier professional development writing efforts led to books for research managers in university settings (Smith, 1986), graduate students in the sciences (Smith, 1998), and most recently regarding the joys, challenges, and failures that permeate the lives of professionals in myriad settings (Smith, 2005). I have dubbed the joys, challenges, and failures phenomena: Pedestals, Parapets, and Pits (3Ps)—in that order.

Pedestals, Parapets, and Pits as Metaphors

Pedestals serve as a metaphor for the glories of professional life. When you are successful, when events around you seem to be humming, when people seem to value what you do and seek you out—you feel the joys of a successful professional life.

Parapets, on the other hand, serve as metaphors for what happens when you and your professional surroundings change and possibly begin to sour. When you are less frequently consulted, when your ideas are less often quoted, when your colleagues seem a bit on edge to be in your presence—then you know the challenges of professional life.

Pits, in a third dimension, are metaphors for the professional life in jeopardy. When you are no longer consulted, when your ideas are ignored, when you are shunned—then you experience the failures of professional life.

The Pedestals of Professional Life

The pedestals of professional life consist primarily of leadership skills and a dedication to professional development—by you, your direct reports, and colleagues. Thus, under the heading of pedestals, I include

- **Communication and Communication Skills:** listening, speaking and writing (see chapters 1–4, 7, 10–12)
- **Service to Direct Reports:** ensuring professional development and reinforcing efforts on a daily basis (see chapters 1, 3, 13–16)
- **Strategic Planning:** envisioning, developing, and implementing strategic plans (see chapter 17)
- **Diversity:** promoting understanding and diversity in the workplace through articulation, commitment, and education (see chapter 9)
- **Integrated Professionalism:** crafting a personal outlook, seeking interdisciplinary connections and insuring lifelong learning (chapter 7)

Several of these topics—directed towards the world of academic administration—have been covered herein as noted above.

To bring the pedestals, parapets, and pits concepts to life, I sought collaboration with an artist who would be able to create cartoon characters and illustrate scenarios of the 3Ps' model of professional life. I found that collaboration with Dusty Higgins, graphic artist for the *Arkansas Democrat-Gazette.* His portrayals of Mr. Pedestals (center), Mr. Parapets (left) and Mr. Pits (right) appear below.

To exemplify Mr. Pedestals's dedication to professional development through pedestal-like values and behavior, Dusty came up with the following:

The Parapets and Pits of Professional Life

In contrast to the concept of pedestals, parapets represent challenges or pivotal moments, which can either stimulate a rededication to pedestal-type efforts *or* lead to the pits or failures of professional life. To characterize the pivotal nature of parapets and their pairing with corresponding pits, Dusty has portrayed Mr. Parapets and Mr. Pits as follows:

The Messrs. Parapets and Pits and other character portrayals through-out the 3Ps book provide sometimes whimsical and sometimes poignant illustrations for the sobering but important pairs of characteristics and failings—parapets and pits respectively—as noted below:

Ambiguity and Apathy: Thoughtful assessments and analyses of chal-lenging situations require tolerance of the parapet *ambiguity,* but if tol-erance leads to long lapses in action, ambiguity may be perceived as the pit of *apathy.*

Ambition and Aggression: *Ambition* is a necessary parapet for profes-sionals whether it plays out in terms of personal career goals or the pursuit of goals and objectives of a firm, institution, or organization; however, when ambition morphs into *aggression*—perhaps through intervening anger, avarice, ignorance, impatience, rudeness, or some combination thereof, one observes *aggression* as one of the pits of pro-fessional of life.

Jealousy and Envy: Although used interchangeably and often erro-neously, *jealousy* and *envy* differ greatly in their effects on others; to wit, *jealousy* as parapet may actually stimulate positive imitative behavior, while if transformed into the pit of *envy,* actions detrimental to others ensue.

Egoism and Narcissism: The parapet *egoism*—a driving force toward self-actualization—fuels creativity and productivity but when manifest through the pits of vanity, conceit, and *narcissism,* personal and work-place damage results.

Drama and Manipulation: The parapet of *drama* adds spice to life and the professional environs, but when used as a stage for the pit of *manip-ulation*—covert or overt—tragedies occur.

Responsiveness and Arrogance: Thoughtful and timely *responsiveness* to all manner of communications from compliments to criticism—mild to modest to severe—offers a parapet used healthily, but when exercised carelessly, too quickly or after long intervals, the parapet may be perceived as the pit of *arrogance.*

Forthrightness and Anger: The parapet of speaking your mind—or *forthrightness*—can have virtuous foundations but may transpose into the pit of *anger* if exercised hastily, thoughtlessly, or recklessly.

Love and Lust: Beneficent concern for colleagues and direct reports may be interpreted as the parapet of *love* but, when evident in more personal terms or with unwanted affection, the pit of *lust* results.

Selectivity and Prejudice: The parapet manifesting itself as *selectivity* in people or foci is necessary to accomplish goals and objectives of firms, institutions, or organizations, but the selectivity parapet sours when tainted by the pits of bias or *prejudice.*

I recommend further reading (Smith, 2005 and references therein) on the above-noted topics, readings that can be very helpful in dealing with the abundance of professional developmental difficulties that arise in the lives of all academic administrators.

As we wind down this section on offering inspiration and direction, I end with a chapter on one of the most challenging difficulties faced by academic administrators: addressing and dealing with tragedy that may befall faculty, staff, or students. It represents somber stuff but a necessary part of academic administrative life. So let's get on with it.

Tragedies

Preparedness and Responses

Life is mostly froth and bubble.
Two things stand like stone,
Kindness in another's trouble,
Courage in your own.
—Adam Lindsay Gordon (1833–1870), Australian poet

I magine this: You are at a meeting with administrative colleagues, and a secretary interrupts to report that a student and faculty member have just been found dead of gunshots, and it appears that the faculty member may have been at fault. He is Caucasian, the student is initially judged to be an African American female. Following this brief report, your supervisor turns to you and says, "It's in your area—you better take the lead." Sound too exaggerated to be true? Well, it happened to me and it happened on the first day of classes in my first year as provost at the University of Arkansas.

Not to keep you in suspense, following is a summary of the incident, which occurred coincidently just four days after my orientation session at the University of Arkansas Police Department:

- The student, rather than being a female, was a male graduate student (James Easton Kelly) in his thirties. He had recently been dismissed from his program on academic grounds and shot his major advisor three times, then turned the gun on himself and killed himself with a bullet through his heart. The incident occurred over a few minutes (i.e., approximately 12:10 to 12:20 p.m.), including the assailant being confronted by police who shouted through the locked door, of the victim's office—just one minute after three 911 reports (Associated Press, 2000 and Wilson, 2000) of gunshots in a building on campus.

- The victim, John Locke, was a beloved faculty member in comparative literature, who ironically did not vote "aye" in the termination decision affecting the student.
- The student had in his possession ninety-six rounds of hollow point bullets and a receipt documenting that he had purchased fifty of them just forty-seven minutes before the incident. Accompanying the ammunition and the receipt in the student's briefcase were letters from faculty members involved in his studies along with his letter of dismissal from the graduate program (Wilson, 2000).

As noted above, the incident came to conclusion quickly. Thus, there was little danger to other faculty members, students, or staff following Mr. Kelly's suicide since there was no evidence of a conspiracy or accomplices. But, for academic administrators, the lessons learned through this incident underline the importance of emergency preparedness and the need for quick and decisive action following tragedies or other catastrophic events. The preparation for and follow-up to such tragedies and crises are the primary topics of this chapter.

Being Prepared

Most college and universities have emergency plans. If you are an academic administrator, you should be aware of such plans, which may be codified within college or university policies. The plans are generally part of an institutional strategy of anticipating, assessing, responding to, and recovering from tragic events, ranging from the kind of murder-suicide noted above to natural calamities to possible terrorist acts.

When thinking of tragedies and responses, it is important to know what role your office plays within the plans. If you are employed at a college or university that has a police force, this unit will usually coordinate efforts, which are often directed by an emergency operations committee (EOC) or its equivalent. The EOC will typically be composed of the chief academic officer (often appointed as chair of the group), the chief student-affairs officer; police officers; counseling services; environmental safety, health, transportation, and public affairs or relations officers; along with director-level officers from computing services and physical plant or facilities management.

The campus's emergency plan will contain protocols for bringing the EOC together (i.e., with indications of threshold events that trigger the assemblage of the group) to assess situations, respond to needs, and begin recovery operations. In the case of the murder-suicide case noted above, the EOC assembled in the university's police department headquarters for work that lasted for much of the remaining day of the tragedy and the next day. Decisions and assignments for actions were developed collectively and followed up by individual and small-team efforts (e.g., location of next of kin, composition of press releases) between signal events such as news conferences, which totaled five in the particular case noted. The actual follow-up actions and recommendations for responses in a myriad of tragic and catastrophic events are considered in the following section.

What's Next?

After an assessment of the severity of a tragic incident and the need to assemble the EOC—through a collective decision of the institution's chief executive officer (CEO) and safety or police administrators—a series of steps are typically invoked. Besides assembling the EOC, a series of notification protocols will be initiated starting with the deans and other comparable offices throughout the institution using e-mail and telephone. It is important, therefore, that academic administrators from deans to department heads or chairs to directors know about their communication responsibilities among other possible emergency-related duties.

Communications during challenging events should be funneled through a campus communications unit and their chief spokespersons. Unless designated otherwise, academic officials should avoid direct contacts with the press. Rather, the college or university should—through its EOC—organize a series of press conferences to get the word out about apparent present or future dangers.

In the murder-suicide case, it was imperative to see that news was broadcast broadly—especially to students, parents, other relatives, and friends—to ensure understanding that danger to community members was eliminated with the death of the assailant. In other instances where perpetrators of crime are on the loose, timely updates are called for on measures being taken to apprehend alleged or suspected criminals, all coordinated through police authorities lest ongoing investigations be compromised.

In the cases of severe accidents or natural crises, frequent press conferences are called for to assist recovery and relief efforts. Typically, the institution's CEO chairs such news conferences and members of the EOC or CEO's executive team may join him or her.

Once a plan for response and recovery is announced, all campus officials should stand ready to do their part including the advising of faculty members and staff on necessary efforts. I have noticed that mass e-mails to the campus community by the CEO, chief academic officer, or other executive officers, properly coordinated, are extremely helpful in keeping follow-up efforts on track, as well as helping to squelch rumors and mitigate fears. More will be noted about this strategy in chapter 26 on inclement weather policies.

While this book was being written, the United States experienced the worst national catastrophe in its history. Hurricane Katrina's devastation of the U.S. Gulf Coast and Louisiana in particular, fixed mental images that will remain for generations in America's collective consciousness.

One of the great successes and human-interest stories that emerged from the Katrina disaster involves the role that Louisiana State University played in service to victims from New Orleans and other parts of Louisiana, including thousands of students displaced by weather-related damage to campuses in the southern part of the state. The LSU story—involving the providing of educational services to more than 3,000 students, shelter for hundreds of relief workers and media professionals, triage and health services to more than 15,000 thousand refugees and other victims of the storm, and the recovery and care of 1,200 pets—was nothing short of spectacular. Recently, LSU has told its story through a well-crafted book (Bacher et al., 2005) and a six-minute video (*Eye of the Storm* DVD, 2005) that should be required reading and viewing by all academic administrators.

Besides embodying vital information and ideas for planning—even for the worst of national catastrophes—the LSU story has an intriguing theme. Namely, major universities have all the necessary components to serve national disaster-relief efforts, including

- Physical facilities such as sports arenas for serving large numbers of people
- Up-to-date and robust communications equipment and systems
- High-quality and competent human resources with a wide variety of knowledge and skills
- Self-generating power systems
- Secure environments

- High-volume food service and housing operations
- A volunteer ethic within its community

What a wonderful way of thinking about the institutions that many of us serve.

In summary, the prospects of significant human tragedies, including criminal acts, natural disasters, and terrorism-related crises call for specific preparedness and follow-up measures that requires planning and drills and, ultimately, well-coordinated recovery and relief actions, the last of which are typically coordinated through a campus police or safety unit. All planning and preparedness efforts should include clear delineation of the roles of all academic administrators from executive officers to department heads or chairs to directors to faculty members and staff.

During the course of this chapter, we have considered a particular case study to see how the planning and action measures play out on a major university campus. I have also taken the liberty of sharing references to some of the superlative work of the LSU community during the Katrina disaster in the late summer of 2005. I end with a quote from author Bacher and her LSU colleagues (2005):

> Students often see college as a dress rehearsal for life. Perhaps the greatest lesson we learned from Katrina is that there are no dress rehearsals; the best way to get the most difficult jobs done is for hope and humanity to join hands. In the wake of Katrina, we at LSU had a front-row seat on the beauty of that union as it carried us through each difficult day. May it continue to carry us all down the long and winding road to recovery.

This chapter concludes section II on offering inspiration and direction. We now go on to section III and a series of chapters providing guidance to a variety of academic administrative players, starting with deans.

Guidance to Various Academic Administrators and Support Professionals

PREAMBLE

Having considered various approaches to offering inspiration and direction to differing academic constituents, I would now like to review academic administrators' roles and responsibilities, including planning, budgeting, and fund raising. We've touched on the administrative work of provosts, but we should also consider guidance on the roles and responsibilities of deans, department chairs or heads, directors, and administrative support professionals. The guidance is offered in a series of chapters in this section along with concluding chapters on strategic planning and coordinated budgeting, and college- or university-wide planning and development. The chapters, overall, capture some of the best thinking of scholars and professionals across a variety of academic institutions. So, let's get started with a chapter I've titled "Why a Dean?"

Why a Dean?

Groucho: "You're a peach, boy! Now, here is a little peninsula, and
here is a viaduct leading over to the mainland."
Chico: "Why a duck?"
Groucho: "I'm all right. How are you? I say here is a little peninsula,
and here's a viaduct leading over to the mainland."
Chico: "All right. Why a duck?"
Groucho: "I'm not playing Ask-Me-Another. I say, that's a viaduct."
Chico: "All right. Why a duck? Why a why a duck? Why a no chicken?"
                                    —*The Cocoanuts*, Paramount, 1929

Considered to be one of the funniest routines in the Marx Brothers'
filmbook, *The Cocoanuts* repartee between Groucho and Chico
(pronounced *Chick-O*) contains hilarious plays on words including
the classic "Why a duck?" which I have adapted for the titles of a series of
chapters on the roles of various academic players in colleges and universities. The players range from department chairs and heads to directors to
deans to vice-provosts and administrative staff.

While composing these chapters, originally as papers that I shared
with a university academic community through an on-line journal (i.e., *All
Things Academic,* http://libinfo.uark.edu/ata/), I anticipated responses
from faculty members along the lines of "Why should we care?" The proffered reason was that academic administrators and related staff make vital
contributions that are often misunderstood or underappreciated within
the academy.

Yes, I know the cynical old saw that "Administrators may be necessary but they are not important." But clearly, I do not believe this, and my hope is that through this series of chapters we may not only enhance common understanding about the roles and responsibilities of academic administrators and staff but also reinforce commitments to work collaboratively with all of our colleagues.

So, we may ask again, Why a dean? In addressing this question, I suggest that we think about the major roles of deans, the qualities that we should expect that they will bring to their responsibilities, the challenges faced by them, and the value they may bring to colleges and universities or their equivalent. We'll end with some thoughts on how deans should interact with students. So, let's begin.

Roles and Responsibilities

In chapter 4, I suggested that your position in an organization influences not only your roles and responsibilities but also your perspectives and views. Deans serve in that proverbial space, "between a rock and a hard place." On the one hand, the dean must be responsive to his or her associate deans, executive committee, department chairs or heads, faculty members,

students, and staff. On the other hand, a dean must partner with the chief academic officer in not only meshing the vision, mission, and goals of the dean's unit with those of the institution but also serving as a strong advocate for her or his college, school, or equivalent unit. The resulting task is both challenging and demanding but may be facilitated by a clear understanding of the roles and values deans need to bring to their posts and day-to-day activities.

Parallel to a chief academic officer's, a dean's task is primarily to inspire, evaluate, and represent their colleges, schools, or equivalent units. Let's look at each of these roles and responsibilities.

Inspiration

A dean should be a source of inspiration to all the people she or he serves. But inspiration and encouragement must come with a dose of realism. Just as a college or university cannot be all things to all people, no dean-led unit can afford to develop all that is potentially possible. Rather the dean—especially when it comes to new program development—must exercise caution in his or her encouragement.

A guiding value or principle for inspiration is quality. Thus, it will be better to develop fewer programs well than achieve mediocrity across many programs. This philosophy and mode of action can be sources of disappointment because chairs and faculty members tend to be ambitious when it comes to program development. The dean is the moderating force—emphasizing the overall importance of quality balanced against need, cost, centrality, and uniqueness. Also, the dean must be aware of and a champion for interdisciplinary or cross-departmental and cross-college or school initiatives that may build on complementary strengths of differing units.

Following the initiation of new programs and indeed during the assessment of current programs, deans play vital roles in evaluation processes.

Evaluation

Academic programs, curricula, and syllabi are the prerogative of the faculty. However, deans (and department chairs and heads) serve in vital roles in evaluating programs and, for that matter, faculty members as well. During such processes, the dean should be the quality-assurance player, making sure that policies are adhered to (especially in tenure and promotion cases) and committees or other faculty bodies are established to test whether standards are met. The evaluations are important whether accreditation organizations are involved or not. And, the fairness and documentation associated with evaluations are critical, particularly given the litigiousness across the national landscape.

Beyond evaluations of programs, faculty, and staff, deans must be the chief stewards of college, school, or equivalent unit resources. This stewardship requires budget preparations and negotiations with the chief academic officer, along with a commitment to the balancing of budgets each and every year. As a chief academic officer my typical message to deans has been this: "I do not need to know all the details of how you are spending unit funds; and, in general, I trust your judgments on expenditures. While this level of control involves considerable tolerance of decisions at the college or school level, there is one thing I do not tolerate and it is 'red ink.'" Overall, I have been pleased during my tenure as a chief academic officer that deans generally understood university policies and my positions on budgets and expenditures and abided by budgetary requirements.

As suggested earlier, a key factor for deans in their evaluation of academic programs is trust. Department chairs or heads and cognizant faculty members must trust the judgment of their dean. Accordingly, it is important for deans to establish effective means of communication with faculty members and groups of faculty. Regular meetings with chairs or heads and periodic meetings with faculty bodies are important vehicles for deans to share information and seek feedback on new programs or initiatives.

Beyond regularly organized meetings, deans should consider retreats where more extended and philosophic discussions can be mounted, especially relative to planning. In smaller collegiate units, retreats can include the entire faculty. Larger colleges may organize retreats at the departmental level or include two or more departments with complementary curricula or goals (e.g., fine arts departments).

Retreats are ideally held off-campus where faculty and administrators are not so prone to day-to-day distractions. At least in some instances, campus continuing-education units can provide facilities for such activities.

Beyond communications, deans build trust with their faculties through collective decisions made over a period of time. Through discussions and decision making, it should be signaled that the dean is not only even-handed, compassionate, and thorough but also capable of making tough choices. Regarding the last, deans must develop the backbone necessary to say "no" when it is called for. If a proposed course of action is unwise or in violation of policy, it is better to cut it off early as opposed to allowing protracted discussions. It need not be an authoritarian "no." Rather, a denial based on a sound rationale ultimately supports the bond of trust between decanal and faculty colleagues.

Once a track record has emerged for a new dean and his or her unit, it will be important for the dean to tackle the next big role and responsibility— namely, representation.

Representation

Deans are the chief spokespersons for their colleges, schools, or equivalent units. Thus, colleges and universities rely on deans for development projects, especially those related to fund-raising and public-relations efforts and problem solving for difficulties that cannot be solved exclusively at departmental levels. To function as a representative, deans must have impeccable integrity, not only for the sake of their collegiate units but also for the overall benefit of the university.

To represent their units well, deans need to hone their communication skills—particularly those related to public speaking. As a chief academic officer, I have taken personal pride in witnessing a dean who represented her or his college or school well. Effective representation is also immensely important to successful initiatives—whether they be for grants, gifts, or programs. And, not least of all, effective representation engenders support for unit proposals through the chief academic officer and other officers in the administration.

To summarize up to this point, deans are primarily charged with inspiration, evaluation, and representation of colleges, schools, or equivalent units. To serve those roles well requires commitments to quality, trust, and integrity. The responsibilities are discharged primarily in service to their faculty groups and the chief academic officer. But, before leaving this topic, it is well to say something about special relationships deans should have with students.

Interactions with Students

Faculty members, departmental chairs and heads, and staff are all key players in serving students of colleges and universities. However, deans have unique opportunities to serve student needs and goals, and it is important for our decanal colleagues to consider such roles seriously.

During my academic administrative career in four research universities, I have been involved in reviews of at least ten deans. In the course of such reviews (i.e., typically completed every five years) questions to students invariably include, "What is your opinion of the effectiveness of your dean?" or more pointedly, "How has your dean affected your program at the university?" Embarrassingly, I have witnessed responses such as "I have no idea who my dean is!" or "I have never met my dean."

Now, it would be unreasonable to expect a dean to know every student in his or her college, school, or equivalent unit. However, it is not unreasonable for a dean to have significant visibility among her or his unit's student body. When this expectation was made clear, I have known several deans who developed student advisory groups that they met with monthly or at least once per semester or quarter.

Deans may also come in contact with students through seminars, all college or school symposia, and awards ceremonies. The effective dean will volunteer to contribute to such efforts if for no other reason than to have opportunities to communicate directly with students.

As suggested previously, deans also play a special adjudicatory role in cases of serious student concerns or grievances. While often challenging, such concerns or grievances present opportunities for deans to display many of the essential talents described earlier.

Dealings with students—as with the myriad other interactions common in the lives of deans—represent time well spent and when coupled with all else expected of deans can fill one's plate. However, there is one additional activity that should be considered by deans, namely, research or scholarly pursuits. In my experience, the most effective and personally and professionally fulfilled deans are those who have scholarly interests that they pursue, taking some nominal percentage of their time. For some deans, particularly those who were educated and trained in the laboratory sciences, such scholarly goals present significant challenges—not least of all, the significant infrastructure support necessary to maintain a program in the sciences or engineering. An additional liability is the real or apparent need to use college or school resources to maintain or upgrade a laboratory.

A wise dean once said, "If you become a dean, never put yourself in the position of competing for resources among your own faculty." Thus, without a substantial endowment (e.g., endowed professorship or chair), science or engineering deans may take on unusual challenges in pursuing their research or scholarly goals. Nevertheless, such challenges can be approached in a variety of ways, and it has always been my wish as chief academic officer that deans contribute to scholarly endeavors in the course of their administrative service. Scholarly endeavors, pursued as part of a team, or indeed independent efforts in areas such as the arts, humanities, and social sciences and in professional development represent highly desirable goals.

Besides being of potential value to executive officers and deans, I hope this chapter, including references that have been helpful in developing my general knowledge of deans and their place in the academy (Bright and Richards, 2001; Martin, 1988; Rosovsky, 1990; Tucker, 1991; and Wolverton et al., 2000), may be useful to faculty who are possibly contemplating a future move to administration. For those faculty members who aspire to transition to a department chair or head position, I offer the advice contained in the next chapter.

Why a Chair or Head?

Most chairs come to their positions without leadership training, without prior administrative experience, and without a clear understanding of their role.

—WALTER H. GMELCH (1947–) and VAL D. MISKIN
(1944–), higher-education scholars

This chapter's title may suggest a gathering of objects for a Marc Chagall or Salvatore Dali painting, but, in actuality, it relates to individuals who many believe are the most critical players in the academy. In the next few pages, we'll explore the definitions of "chairs" and "heads"—including how these posts are typically addressed through college and university policies and the roles and responsibilities of chairs and heads—and at end, consider some suggestions that may assist faculty in transitioning into and out of departmental leadership positions. But, let's begin with some definitions.

Chair or Head?

We all know that a department chair or head is the person charged with administering an academic department. But, few academics are familiar with perceptions about the differences between chairs and heads.

In 2005 I polled the academic deans at the University of Arkansas and sought their views on the difference between department chairs and heads. I wanted to determine how the deans' understandings meshed with what I had encountered at other universities.

A chair is often perceived as a choice of the faculty, but chairs are clearly appointed by a dean. A head, on the other hand, is perceived as principally the appointee of the dean, but deans clearly acknowledge that department heads would not be appointed without input from relevant faculty. These notions are consistent with those I have observed at other universities, although—as will be noted later—the literature on departmental leadership tends to focus exclusively on the term of "department chair."

Frequently, chairs are chosen from within departments, while department heads are often recruited extramurally. However, there may be no college or university policy requiring either approach; thus a variety of factors enters into hiring practices, including the educational opportunities and missions of departments and collegiate units and the needs of a college or university, all of which should receive consideration.

Regardless of whether they serve as chairs or heads, the individuals assuming these roles are the principal administrative officers of academic departments. The jobs possess a set of roles and responsibilities that places them "in the middle"—between faculty and deans. Thus, they face challenges similar to those of deans but with a different range of core roles and responsibilities. Let's continue with a look at these roles and responsibilities.

Roles and Responsibilities of Chairs and Heads

Because of their academic frontline positions, chairs and heads (for simplicity, hereafter referred to generically as "chairs") assume major responsibility for the professional development of their departments' faculty members. As formidable as that faculty-development responsibility may be—by itself—chairs have other significant roles.

In their book on chairing an academic department, Gmelch and Miskin (2004) define the primary roles and responsibilities of chairs as managing, leading, developing faculty, and studying (i.e., personal research and scholarship). Lucas (1994), in her book on strengthening department leadership, also espouses the importance of the four previously noted roles and responsibilities and further notes that faculty members contemplating the assumption of chairs' positions are probably least prepared to assume the leadership and faculty development roles. Other books and articles (e.g., Tucker, 1993 and Seagren et al., 1993 and references cited in both) confirm the importance of the aforementioned roles and responsibilities, so let's consider them one at a time—in the order suggested by Gmelch and Miskin (2004).

The Chair as Manager

Departments are organized for teaching, research and scholarship, and service to the college or university community and society. The day-to-day fulfilling of these commitments requires of a chair skills as manager. The chair must tend to the needs and concerns of students, manage budgets, develop class schedules and assignments, and organize departmental functions. The efforts also include the supervision of departmental staff and the maintenance of facilities and equipment.

In my view, the academic manager's most important responsibilities revolve about student needs and concerns and budgets. Student needs and concerns should always have the highest priority whether they involve developing sufficient numbers of course sections to meet demand, providing effective advising, or addressing specific concerns about course delivery.

Budgets need focused care and attention to prevent deficits and effectively use resources. Budgetwise, chairs need to consider partnerships with deans or other unit administrators to leverage resources and should devote time to the development of compelling justifications for increased funding. When the student- and budget-related efforts are added to the chair's other managerial roles and responsibilities, it is generally found that the overall responsibilities as manager—consume the largest percentage of a chair's time (Gmelch and Miskin, 2004).

Academic managerial efforts are not unlike the management of units in other sectors in society, and preparing oneself for this aspect of the chair's job can be sought through the references noted earlier along with references of a more general nature. For example, the American Management Association (AMA), through its "e-learning" program, offers Internet-based courses with titles such as "Communication Skills," "Human Resources," "Management Skills," "Professional Development," and "Project Management." Additionally, the AMA offers print-version self-study courses in the areas of "First Line Supervision," "How to Manage Conflict in the Organization," "Leadership Skills for Managers," and "Taking Control with Time Management" (American Management Association, 2005). Many colleges and universities, also offer relevant management-oriented programs.

Regardless of how effective managerial skills are acquired, they are necessary and worth some time to develop.

Management involves efforts that relate principally to the present. Leadership, on the other hand, entails efforts that relate primarily to the future (Kouzes and Posner, 1989). Let's consider the chair's leadership roles and responsibilities next.

The Chair as Leader

Leadership is about insuring a better tomorrow. Thus, departments with strong leaders are actively and continually involved with strategic planning. The planning helps to shape understanding about the vision, mission, overarching goals, and objectives of departments. Most importantly, academic leaders help departmental faculty and staff focus on strengths—identifying areas where the department can excel in teaching, research, and service.

As a part of my academic administrative duties, I have visited dozens of academic departments. During these visits, I typically ask department chairs to offer an overview of their units, including plans, which should have references to foci of excellence. It has often been surprising to learn that planning and discussions of planning are apparently accorded less than optimal attention among some academic departments. When it has been my place to do so, my message in follow-up conversations with relevant deans would be that we all understand the crush of day-to-day demands on chairs and their faculty and staff, but it is important for departmental-level units to engage seriously in planning. Moreover, departmental planning should emphasize a meshing of college or school and university goals with those developed in departmental units.

Beyond planning for their departments, effective chairs should act as agents of change in collegiate and university forums and activities. By this I mean that the chairs—those who are capable leaders—should be contributing ideas and volunteering efforts at college- and university-levels, particularly as such efforts involve interdisciplinary programs in teaching and research. Additionally, leadership is reflected in innovations that chairs bring to departmental initiatives, organizational structures, and operations.

The leadership of chairs is also manifested in the collegial climate developed within departments. Outstanding chairs help to set the tone for the department—by example and through communications and meetings—a tone of openness to ideas and healthy debate, all of which should take place in a culture of respect for diversity and divergent views, due process, fairness, and integrity that strengthens departments and contributes positively to interactions among faculty, staff, and students.

We made the distinction earlier about a chair's managerial role being related principally to the present versus the chair's leadership efforts focusing on the future. The chair's third function—development of faculty members—brings the present and future efforts of a department together in critically important ways. Let's consider this synthesis next.

The Chair as Contributor to Faculty Development

There is an apocryphal story about Milton Eisenhower when he served as president of Johns Hopkins University. Allegedly, during a state-of-the-university speech, a faculty member interrupted Eisenhower following his comment regarding the university being "all about students." The faculty member's retort was "The University is the faculty—period!" While the story is about extreme positions, the truth is one cannot have a great college or university without great faculty, and chairs play a major role in the recruitment, development, and retention of great faculty—singly and collectively. Let's consider some critical aspects of faculty recruitment, development, and retention relative to the responsibilities of chairs.

Recruitment of faculty is an everpresent responsibility of chairs. Even in years when there are no openings in departments, chairs can never be sure when faculty members may decide to retire or be recruited by other institutions. Accordingly, effective chairs are well networked with colleagues in their discipline and are constantly on the lookout for talent while attending national and international meetings.

Attention to recruitment and its prospects should also be interlaced with efforts to enhance the diversity of faculty and staff within units. Such efforts require a good understanding of affirmative-action policies and diversity efforts as organized through the college's or university's human resources unit, office of affirmative action, and perhaps special diversity units organized through offices of the chief executive or academic officers.

Recruitment of great faculty for a department is not the end of a chair's responsibility relative to the development of faculty. Once on board, faculty members need support and further development regardless of their background and experience. Faculty at the assistant professor level especially need guidance in honing their teaching skills and in developing creative, research, and scholarly programs. Effective chairs will assist new faculty to connect with teaching- and faculty-support centers and offices of research and sponsored programs or their equivalent units. Chairs should also assume responsibility for assisting new assistant professors in choosing a mentor or mentors to best ensure success towards promotion and tenure.

The best chairs understand promotion, tenure, and posttenure review systems inside and out, including current policies at the department, college, university, and system levels, as relevant. Effective chairs also know when consultation with their deans and other members of the academic chain of command is warranted. In short, through the regular review of and the development of understanding of tenure and promotion policies and procedures, chairs become of great help to faculty members' advancement and development.

Chairs should also understand the stresses that accompany the development and advancement of highly accomplished individuals. And, when such stresses turn into disagreements or grievances, chairs should know how to help parties resolve their differences and how to access professional help that is available on- and off-campus.

Beyond the formal attention to faculty development, good chairs know that departmental harmony and esprit de corps emanate from a variety of efforts that enhance day-to-day morale and goodwill among faculty and staff. The development of newsletters to enhance communications, the crafting of events to acknowledge individual and departmental achievements, and simple acts of personal acknowledgement of faculty accomplishments all have great value, as every successful chair knows.

At this point, you might be asking, Given all the above-noted roles and responsibilities, is there any time left for the effective chair to consider her or his continued development as a scholar? To which, I would respond, Chairs have to make time for personal scholarship. Let's consider this topic next.

The Chair as Scholar

Prospective chairs are often identified and appointed because of their exemplary teaching and scholarly skills and accomplishments. However, as may have been gleaned from the above, it takes a lot more than teaching and scholarly expertise to be an effective chair. Nevertheless, the most effective chairs know that their academic life will continue after they are chair, and even if they contemplate a move to other administrative posts, they are best served if their scholarly lives advance throughout administrative stints. The trick is to find balance and to leverage opportunities that present themselves.

In the previous chapter, in the discussion of the scholarly efforts of deans, I referred to how difficult it can be for deans to pursue their research and scholarship, particularly in laboratory-based disciplines. Such challenges also exist for chairs, although perhaps somewhat less than that for deans. But, because of their positions, chairs have enhanced opportunities for collaboration with other faculty, and these opportunities—along with scholarly pursuits that dovetail directly with administrative responsibilities—should represent viable options for chairs.

The literature on chairing academic departments is replete with references to the challenges chairs face in finding the time to continue their scholarly pursuits while seeking excellence in their roles as chairs. I suggest that chairs and other administrators have no choice, lest they wish to become stagnant or worse—suffer burnout through their administrative lives. In short, it is essential for chairs to make time to advance their scholarship. In this regard, I emphasize the broad definition of scholarship espoused by Boyer (1990) that includes discovery, integration, application, and teaching, all of which nurture academic souls. Furthermore, I suggest that all faculty—be they mainstream or administrative types—make time each day to pursue scholarship in one or more of its forms. For a poet, like Maya Angelou, it might be just finding "a word." For other scholars and researchers, it may be composing a paragraph. For still others, it may be crafting a talk or a lecture. But, chairs' focusing on administrative duties to the exclusion of scholarship should not be an option.

Summarizing to this point, we've considered the definitions of "chairs" and "heads" and their roles and responsibilities in the areas of managing, leading, and developing faculty and pursing scholarship. At this chapter's end, I offered a plea that regardless of administrative roles or commitments all academics engage in productive scholarship throughout their professional lives. Scholarly pursuits are key to successful careers—whether they involve advancement administratively or returning to fulltime faculty posts.

We now move on to what may be the least understood of academic administrator posts—that of director.

Why a Director?

Here physicists, chemists, and biologists really live together. They aren't just placed together, they work and think together.

"Team" isn't the right word. You don't decide, "we're going to have a team"—at least I don't. You look at the problems, what has to be done, and who can do it. Pretty soon, people start getting together. . . . They're wiling to take the trouble to participate in their neighbors' concerns. Really participate, not just advise. That's an important distinction.

—MELVIN CALVIN (1911–1997), scientist, Nobel laureate, and
long-term director of the Laboratory of Chemical
Biodynamics, University of California Berkeley

The title of this chapter may conjure up visions of leaders of orchestras or theater companies, but it relates to individuals who play a variety of interesting roles in the academy. We'll look at heads of schools, academic programs, organized research units, and administrative service and outreach units—all under the heading of "director." We'll review how some directors serve in roles and responsibilities that parallel those of deans or department chairs, while those connected with research units take on highly creative roles, while directors of service units sometimes act principally as managers with strong personnel development responsibilities. We'll begin with some context for the somewhat elusive term of "director."

Director of What?

As suggested above, "director" is a term universities use to designate the head of a school, program, or organized research, administrative service, or outreach unit. Let's consider each—briefly.

At many universities, one finds schools that are led by deans, who report to a chief academic officer. This administrative arrangement is typical for schools that represent focused professional areas such as in architecture and law. For a graduate school, the title "school" is inconsistent with the arguments noted below about the use of the terms "schools" versus "colleges," but is congruent with the title's use in numerous universities, as will be reinforced below.

You may now be asking, What then is the difference between a school and a college? Here is where some confusion comes in. Seek a dictionary set of descriptions and you'll find considerable overlap among the definitions of "college" and "school." But, you'll find the title "school" commonly associated with smaller academic units while the term "college" tends to be used for larger academic units, notwithstanding the common designation "graduate school," which represents sizable numbers of students who pursue their degrees in concert with programs primarily based in other colleges and schools. The "schools" versus "colleges" terminology is somewhat arcane and may represent one of several reasons people sometimes become confused about academic organizational structures and operations.

To summarize up to this point, schools tend to be smaller academic units; colleges are larger and more diverse academic units. Thus we note that most university-based arts and sciences and academic business units are designated as "colleges."

Adding to academic administrative complexity, however, is the realization that "schools" may be imbedded within colleges. Thus, at some universities, you will find

- Schools of social work organized within colleges of arts and sciences
- Schools of nursing imbedded in colleges of education and health professions or their equivalents
- Schools of human environmental sciences (i.e., typically offering areas of study such as apparel design, development, and merchandizing; hospitality studies; human development; interior design; and nutrition) contained within colleges of agriculture and agriculture and home economics or their equivalents

Leaders of schools within colleges typically bear the title "director." And, in many institutions—for cases similar to the ones noted above—the schools' directors would report to the deans of their colleges.

Now, you may be musing, I know of universities that have colleges or schools of social work, nursing, and human environmental sciences with deans who report to the chief academic officers of the institutions. What influences the difference in the designation and on what bases might switches be made in reporting responsibilities? Typically, cases are made by representative units for changes in reporting responsibilities or "school" versus "college" designations based on the size, complexity, and missions of the academic units in question.

In addition to schools, faculty members may also be appointed as directors of academic programs that transcend academic departments. Thus, at a number of institutions, you will find director-led programs such as,

- African American studies, comparative literature, and medieval studies
- Interdisciplinary biotechnology, photonics, and public-policy doctoral programs in graduate schools
- Honors programs in the schools and colleges
- And many more

Risking further potential confusion, let's consider the title of "director" in another context, namely the leader of a research unit. I like the term, "organized research units" or ORUs to denote a series of units that bear the titles laboratories, offices, centers, and institutes—developed in that hierarchical order and for the purposes of advancing and facilitating academic research and scholarship in areas that typically cut across traditional academic disciplines. Thus, at different institutions, you will find ORUs with names such as,

- The Arkansas Center for Space and Planetary Sciences at the University of Arkansas
- The Center for the Study of Religion and Conflict at Arizona State University
- The Roper Center of Public Opinion Research at the University of Connecticut
- The Drug Dynamics Institute at the University of Texas at Austin
- The Center for the Humanities at the University of Wisconsin-Madison

- Institute for Shock Physics at Washington State University
- And many, many more

Laboratories, offices, centers, and institutes are typically organized under college and university umbrellas and are usually led by a person who bears the title "director." Directors of such units may report to department chairs or heads, associate deans, deans, or upper-level administrators such as vice-provosts for research.

Beyond the director-led schools and academic and research programs noted above, there are administrative service and outreach units that are headed by professionals with the title of "director." Thus, for example, you will find directors leading

- Offices of admissions, institutional research, and student financial aid
- Advancement, financial, and student affairs centers, offices, and programs
- Centers for mathematics and science education, offices of research and sponsored programs, and testing services units
- And many, many more

At this point, some may be thinking, Whew, do we need all these directors? While individual units are always subject to assessment and reconfiguration, the number of director-led units is often justifiable given the complexity of many higher-education institutions. Indeed, I often allude to U.S. universities as communities with missions more complex and multifaceted than that of many state agencies, cities, and towns within any given state. More succinctly, administrative leadership and management structures are necessary to make complex and diverse communities function effectively. Considering the latter functions and keeping in mind that directors serve at the discretion of their supervisors, let's explore the specific roles and responsibilities of directors in units across the teaching, research, and academic service spectrum of a typical college or university.

What Are the Roles and Responsibilities of Directors of Schools?

As noted earlier, directors may serve as unit leaders of college-based schools with teaching, research, and service missions akin to their college counterparts. In such units, it is common for the directors to report to deans.

Director-led schools are infrequently organized into departments. Accordingly, these school directors have responsibilities that overlap with those of chairs or heads and, to a degree, those of deans. Recalling the fourfold roles and responsibilities of chairs or heads (i.e., managing, leading, developing faculty, and personal scholarship) and the tripartite roles and responsibilities of deans (i.e., inspiration, evaluation, and representation), one can imagine significant challenges for college-based school directors. However, we recognize the size differentials that often exist between college-based schools and colleges within universities.

Nevertheless, the importance of college-based school directors requires careful consideration relative to appointment and continued service. Once appointed, directors need to recognize their broad-based administrative and managerial roles and responsibilities and consider opportunities for continued education and development.

School-level directors' roles and responsibilities bear some resemblance to that of academic program directors but there are some distinct differences for the latter as we shall see next.

What Are the Roles and Responsibilities of Directors of Academic Programs?

Academic programs, be they interdisciplinary (e.g., African American studies program within a college of arts and sciences) or curriculum based (e.g., college- or school-based honors programs), typically engage leaders with the title "director," as noted earlier. In contrast to the director of a college-based school, academic program directors lead units that are not permanent homes for tenured and tenure-track faculty; thus such directors generally have more limited faculty development responsibilities than directors of schools or chairs and heads of traditional academic departments. However, this fact does not lessen the need for interpersonal and communication skills for director-level appointees. Indeed, leaders of interdisciplinary and other broad-based units often require extraordinary interpersonal and communication skills in order to engage faculty and staff members across sometimes disparate units.

While the roles and responsibilities of academic program directors will vary according to the type of program, these directors need to develop goals and objectives in concert with their faculty and staff—goals and objectives that are consistent with the vision articulated by collegiate unit deans or associate deans. On top of these challenges, is the fact that programs of the type noted rarely have substantial budgets; thus it behooves academic program directors to be creative in seeking extramural funding for projects and initiatives. This latter effort becomes even more important for directors of ORUs—as we'll consider next.

What Are the Roles and Responsibilities of Directors of Organized Research Units?

ORU directors play vital roles in colleges and universities, and most especially in research universities. Given the highly interdisciplinary nature of much modern research and scholarship and given the shared nature of complex and expensive research instrumentation—especially in the sciences and engineering—and given the importance of extramural funding in most areas of research and scholarship, ORU directors have their work cut out for them. And, beyond the roles and responsibilities inherent in the above-noted features, ORU directors are further responsible for the strategic planning and interdepartmental and interinstitutional collaborations that make modern research and scholarly efforts productive.

If you talk with the directors of the ORU types mentioned above, I know that they would refer to the challenges articulated in this section. Additionally, and like academic program leaders, ORU directors would undoubtedly emphasize the relatively modest permanent budgets in place to support their efforts. Similarly, they will emphasize how important extramural funding is to their operations and the future of their units; thus, they will have to have keen grant-writing skills and capabilities. Additionally, since large grants necessitate cooperation and collaboration with many faculty members and other institutions, being an ORU director requires well-honed interpersonal and communication skills.

Some ORUs will have staff members with ongoing appointments to meet unit missions. Thus, responsible directors will need to be good managers, including attention to professional development matters. The personnel development piece is especially critical for academic and service unit directors who we will consider next.

What Are the Roles and Responsibilities of Directors of Academic and Administrative Service and Outreach Units?

One cannot imagine fulfilling the missions of colleges or universities without a range of administrative service and outreach units such as admissions, continuing education, research support and sponsored programs, registrar, and student financial aid—among many others. For universities and particularly research universities, units of the type noted typically have sizable annual budgets and significant numbers of exempt or nonclassified and nonexempt or classified staff members. The directors' roles and responsibilities relate to goals and objectives developed at the university level and affect the institution as a whole.

In general, administrative service and outreach unit directors take on considerable responsibilities for the efficient performance of their units. Frequently, they do their work with tight budgets and limited resources for salaries, thereby necessitating that administrative service and outreach unit directors take a keen interest in staff development, including the crafting of plans and initiatives to fund staff support.

Having considered the roles and responsibilities of a wide array of administrative service and outreach directors and recognizing that they face great challenges—not least of all operating with modest institution budgets—you may be wondering, Why does anybody want to assume any of these jobs? The answer lies largely in what management experts iterate over and over about the assumption of challenging managerial and administrative positions: the opportunity to make a difference—especially in situations where the stakes are high and the returns are great (e.g., educating and training the next generation of leadership for our nation)—offers powerful motivations for dedication and service.

In summary, we've considered directors and their roles and responsibilities in units from schools to academic programs to organized research units to administrative service and outreach operations. It is now time to move on to the last of the "Why a . . ." chapters with consideration given to administrative support professionals.

CHAPTER 16

Why Administrative Support Professionals?

When I look back upon my early days, I am stirred by the thought of the number of people I have to thank for what they gave me or for what they were to me. . . . I think we all live spiritually, by what others have given us in the significant hours of our lives.

—ALBERT SCHWEITZER (1875–1965),
philosopher, physician and theologian

We all need administrative support. Whether you serve as chief academic officer, dean, or chair of a department, the need for support personnel becomes apparent quickly unless you work at a very small institution or academic unit. This chapter deals with the roles and responsibilities and administrative skills and capabilities of support staff from vice-provosts or associate provosts to associate deans, associate or vice-chairs, and chief administrative assistants—commonly titled as "assistant-to" professionals. We'll end with some suggestions for serving the staff development needs of these vital players of the academy.

Chief Academic Officer Associates

Depending on the title of a chief academic officer (e.g., provost, vice-president or vice-chancellor for academic affairs or some combination thereof) one commonly encounters associated staff with titles such as vice-provost for _____ (i.e., substitute appropriate descriptor such as "academic affairs" or "research"), associate vice-chancellor for _____ (i.e., with appropriate descriptor such as "academic affairs" or "research") or associate provost. These associates are typically professionals who come from the faculty ranks of the parent institution and are usually tenured and have the rank of "professor." Faculty rank is important to ensure proper respect for the associate as he or she builds relationships with the faculty.

In larger universities, chief academic officers will require at least two associates to help handle matters related to the crucial areas of academic affairs and research. For the former, the chief academic officer may not only assign certain responsibilities to the associates (e.g., acting as liaison with state departments of higher education in cases of public institutions, revision and updating of academic policies) but also rely on the associate to handle certain casework that flows through all academic affairs offices. Associates' prior service and experience are critical to the roles noted because of the need for institutional memory, particularly in cases where chief academic officers have been recruited from other institutions. I am fond of relating an anecdote to friends and colleagues: akin to guerrilla warfare—when you parachute into a new institution as an academic administrator, to be successful as a "newcomer," it is essential to surround yourself with competent associates (or "friendlies") who know how to "work effectively through the system."

Besides an associate in academic affairs, the chief academic officer of a university needs an associate in research who most often serves as the chief research officer for the institution.

The chief research officer may or may not come from the institution's faculty, but should—akin to the academic affairs associate—have tenure and be appointed at the level of professor. In my experience, chief research officers frequently have backgrounds in the sciences, mathematics, or engineering because of the nature of the challenges of the job relative to institutional and extramurally funded research. Some social scientists and humanists may adapt to the world of academic research administration, although their learning curves are likely to be steeper than those colleagues who come from the natural sciences and engineering.

Chief research officers serve in more than helping roles in research development. In fact, they typically serve as chief state and federal compliance officers for a myriad of areas from animal and human subjects research to the handling of radioisotopes and biohazards to research mis-

conduct, to name just a few. Chief research officers are also commonly in oversight positions for offices of sponsored programs (or their equivalent), which typically handle the official review of grant proposals and extramural awards including project reports required by external agencies as well as oversight of compliance committees (Institutional Review Board, Institutional Animal Care and Use Committee). Again, having the respect of faculty members and research staff will be crucial to the successful functioning of chief research officers.

While the compliance duties of chief research officers may be officially delegated by an institution's chief executive officer, the day-to-day consultations in such matters will typically fall under the purview of chief academic officers.

Besides associates in academic affairs and research, chief academic officers will frequently have other associates in areas such as continuing education, outreach, diversity, and institutional research, to name just a few. Here also, faculty credentials are vital to the effective functioning of a chief academic officer's associates.

It probably goes without saying that chief academic officer associates need keen communication skills, if for no other reason than to represent well the chief academic officer—as necessary. The associates also need to have the skills of a diplomat to negotiate the contentious matters that commonly flow through academic affairs offices. So, if you are a chief academic officer, choose your associates wisely, as they will provide vital services to your academic affairs unit.

Akin to chief academic officers, deans—particularly those associated with larger colleges or schools—will need associate deans to assist in a myriad of areas. Let's consider these associates next.

Associate Deans

Deans of colleges and schools of moderate size (i.e., 1,000–2,000 students) or larger and moderate complexity (e.g., offering undergraduate and graduate or professional degrees) will find it difficult to function without one or more associate deans. Particularly at a time when deans are being asked to do more in fund raising and development (Wolverton, et al., 2001), associate deans are needed to cover the college or school when deans must engage in related travel.

As the associates of chief academic officers are, associate deans are best suited coming from the faculty ranks and when possible holding tenure and the rank—at a minimum—of associate professor. In cases of colleagues holding the associate professor rank, the appointing dean should face the possibility—head-on—of the likelihood that the associate dean appointment may impede progress of promotion to full professor.

Besides serving in the dean's place, an associate dean may be assigned prescribed responsibilities in academic oversight ranging from advising centers to student recruitment and retention to yearly promotion and tenure procedures to collegiate-based learning and research centers.

The dean and his or her associate deans may also serve as an executive committee of the college or school, perhaps along with budget, development, and communication officers.

In large multifaceted colleges or schools (e.g., arts and sciences, medicine) an associate dean may be appointed as the chief collegiate research officer with roles and responsibilities paralleling those of a university-wide chief research officer.

Akin to chief academic officer associates, associate deans need to have the requisite communication and diplomatic skills to serve in the place of deans as needed. Thus, deans need to take these skills into account before making appointments.

Similar to deans and their associates, chairs of larger departments frequently find a need for associate or vice-chairs, and we'll consider these associates next.

Associate or Vice-Chairs

Departments, especially those in larger colleges or universities, are often complex enough to merit appointment of an associate or vice-chair. The latter may assist in management roles, so the chair may concentrate her or his efforts in leadership and faculty development roles as discussed in chapter 13. I have also observed situations where associate chairs played key roles in budget control and academic assessments.

The chair who is also an active researcher or scholar will value an associate chair who can serve in his or her place when travel is required to keep the chair's scholarly or research program going.

Up to this point, we have considered associates who are peers to chief academic officers, deans, and chairs. Let's now consider the last vital professional of this chapter—those in "assistant to" positions.

Professionals Who Serve in "Assistant-to" Positions

If you have been in academic administration for some time, you already know how important the "assistant-to" professional is in your administrative life. For the novice academic administrator, however, we should consider some background on the importance of the assistant-to professional. I'll begin with a short personal anecdote.

If you were to ask any of the assistant-to professionals who have worked for me in my roles as academic division head, research institute director, academic and graduate deans, chief research officer, and chief academic officer, I hope you would have heard something like, "I served in an assistant-to position for Bob Smith, but all the while I felt like an associate of his." Indeed, that was my intention.

Assistant-to professionals are typically educated at the baccalaureate level or equivalent but need the skills and abilities of associates who often function in seemingly more complex and responsible roles. Additionally, it will be critical for your assistant-to professional to be impeccably trustworthy since she or he will be privy to most if not all of your projects and efforts. How else will he or she maintain your calendar, speak on your behalf, and organize your office to best serve your assigned duties and responsibilities?

I also look for initiative, diligence, and loyalty in assistant-to professionals and can honestly admit that all who have served my offices have demonstrated these attributes. Additionally, all have been trusted friends, and I would dare say—confidants. Thus, I felt comfortable sharing information with assistant-to professionals that I might not share with all other members of my working team, in part, because of the assistant-to's need to know.

As you reflect on all that has been offered in this chapter thus far, you may find yourself musing, Much of what has been noted about professional associates—at all levels—seems idealistic. But, for me, I have nearly unfailingly had associates—at all levels—whom I have valued and trusted. Their loyalty and dedication came in part because of the contributions I tried to make to each and every associate's professional development. Let's consider this capstone topic next.

Professional Development of Associates

The greatest service one can offer to associates is to assist in their professional development. Aiding professional development also has beneficial effects for your institution.

A commitment to professional development requires an understanding of mentoring, the belief in a successor philosophy, and a concern for colleagues' career goals. Let's consider further, each of these commitments.

The concept of mentoring emanates from the great Homeric work, the *Odyssey*, as noted in chapter 6. But, akin to the term's use in other contexts, it also applies well to your intentions with associate-type professionals along with a successor philosophy that we will consider next.

The wise academic administrator knows that life often takes perilous turns, frequently resulting in the incapacitation or loss of a leader. Thus, the thoughtful academic administrator will ensure that potential successors are developed among their associates. The efforts require mentoring as noted earlier and a keen interest in professional development, including support of lifelong learning. You might now be asking about approaches to mentoring and its support of a successor philosophy. For me, mentoring begins with Opulente's prescriptions, which I referred to in chapter 6, and a series of professional development interventions. We will revisit Opulente's prescriptions very shortly, but first allow me to introduce this topic by means of a short story.

When speaking to young professionals about career development, I often use the metaphor of board games, three types of which may be referred to as "clearing-the-board," "rearranging-the-board," and "filling-the-board" games. Practically everyone has had a chance to try all three.

Checkers, chess, and the chess-relative Kriegspiel exemplify clearing-the-board games. Rearranging-the-board games are exemplified by Chinese checkers, Chutes and Ladders, and Parcheesi. Filling-the-board games are represented by Scrabble, the ancient Chinese game of go, and Hex, the latter of which was codeveloped in the United States by John Forbes Nash, the Nobel laureate and principal figure of the story, *A Beautiful Mind* (Nasar, 1998).

Hex is played with a parallelogram-shaped board molded with contiguous hexagon-shaped wells and two opposing black and white sides. Two people play the game as in chess, but the purpose of the game is to fill the board as necessary—in alternating sequence of play—with rhombus-shaped black or white pieces in a continuous line of single colored pieces while preventing your opponent from doing the same. The game is therefore similar to the ancient game of go, but instead of capturing territory, in Hex you attempt to craft continuous, though possibly circuitous lines from one side of the board to another.

As the game proceeds—and as you can imagine because of blocking moves by your opponent—the Hex board typically fills up to a great extent, and the victor is the one who not only can think strategically but also has a keen sense of pattern recognition. Here's where the metaphor for professional development and lifelong learning comes in.

Imagine professionals' life histories in terms of games of Hex—filling in the spaces as they get older, as they learn and grow in wisdom. I often suggest to young colleagues—extending the metaphor a bit further—that they should continually be looking for patterns and interconnected understanding as they grow and mature. I also suggest that in the highly interdisciplinary world of the twenty-first century, the most successful professionals and the most fulfilled human beings will be those who constantly fill in and meaningfully connect the intellectual, emotional, and social components of their lives.

E. O. Wilson (1998), the great Harvard University entomologist and philosopher, might refer to my Hex-game metaphor as "consilience." What Wilson means by "consilience" is the concept that all fields or disciplines are interrelated and all fields of study from the arts to the humanities to the social and natural sciences can assist in crafting a web of understanding that serves us well in professional development. The key to consilience thinking is to consider Opulente's prescriptions, first introduced in chapter 6: 1) continuing education, 2) reading seminal books, and 3) developing an interdisciplinary approach to all you do.

Continuing education plays out in myriad ways from self-directed reading to workshops to membership and participation in professional organizations, as will be noted in the last portion of this section.

The reading of seminal books may seem obvious but some additional reflection is worthwhile.

In his wonderful recent book on leadership, the extraordinarily successful university president Steven Sample (2002) refers to seminal books as "supertexts." We know these books as the *Bible*, the *Bhagavad-Gita*, Dante's *The Divine Comedy*, Plato's *Republic*, Machiavelli's *The Prince*, Shakespeare's *Hamlet* and *Othello*, Thoreau's *Walden*, and the *Tao Te Ching*, to name just a few. They are worth reading and rereading. But, my advice to younger colleagues goes further: Don't stop there! Going back to Professor Opulente's third prescription, I recommend taking advantage of reading and study that brings Sample's supertexts into new light. For me, Carl Sagan's Pulitzer Prize–winning *Dragons of Eden* (1977), Joseph Campbell's *The Hero With a Thousand Faces* (1968), Jared Diamond's Pulitzer Prize–winning, *Guns, Germs, and Steele—The Fates of Human Societies* (1997), and E. O. Wilson's *Consilience* (1998) are among those I would call modern classics, and these modern classics help to illuminate the well-recognized classics in truly interdisciplinary ways.

After developing an understanding of Opulente's prescriptions, I encourage you to develop a plan for further professional and career development of associates, involving the following elements:

■ Short courses and workshops: These can be developed in-house but are also available through a variety of sources from private firms to community colleges to university-based continuing-education operations

■ Professional organization and society involvement: A year should not go by in which associates do not have an opportunity to attend and more importantly, contribute to—through paper presentation, panel participation, or equivalent activity—a regional or national meeting. For assistants-to professionals I particularly recommend membership and participation in the programs of the International Association of Administrative Professionals (http://www.iaap-hq.org/), with six hundred chapters and forty-thousand members or affiliates throughout the world

■ Retreats or other internal meeting participation

■ Cross-training: Ensuring opportunities for associates to broaden their understanding of different segments of your organization by formal and informal cross-training efforts. Such efforts can often be coordinated through others who serve as your direct reports

Summarizing this section, we have considered the value of mentoring, a successor philosophy, and a concern for career goals as critical to the professional development of associates. All of these activities require conscientiousness and reinforcement through daily practices.

Ending this chapter brings to a close a series of chapters with advice on roles, responsibilities, and development of a range of academic administrative officials. We now head off in a new direction to complete this section on guidance to various academic administrators and support professionals with a chapter on strategic planning and budgeting.

Strategic Planning and Budgeting

Strategic planning requires the organization to make an analysis of its potential comparative advantages. Each department in the university should be constructed on a base of comparative advantages. . . . Some may stem from history, others from strength of different departments within the university, and still others from individuals within a department. Occasionally, a comparative advantage may stem from location. . . .

—RICHARD CYERT (1921–1998), professor of economics and president of Carnegie Mellon University from 1972 to 1990

Planning is critical to the vitality of all academic units—be they large or small. Beyond its institutional merit, planning is a wonderful tool for bringing groups of people together. Indeed, what better way might there be to unite people than to have them deal with the future they will live in?

In this chapter we will consider the importance of planning efforts to units within higher-education institutions and to the people that serve them. We'll also consider the elements of strategic planning from vision to environmental assessment to mission to goals and objectives—all with an eye towards meaningful involvement of unit members. Later in the chapter, we will consider how planning should shape actions and the budgets that serve them. But first, let's consider the context for planning—namely, the future.

Considering the Future

People are generally fascinated by the future—conceptually and as it applies to institutions where individuals vested interests lie, where they work. When talking about the future, you can point to its universal appeal and note that while the past is honored by a great number of historically oriented associations, "things to come" is the focus of fewer but still intriguing organizations including the World Future Society (http://www.wfs.org/), which was started in the United States in 1966 and in 2005 had thirty-thousand members in eighty countries around the world. If you are crafting presentations about the future of an organization, you can also include references to notable personages—and their thoughts about this topic. Here are some of my favorites:

> "The best thing about the future is that it comes one day at a time."
> —Abraham Lincoln (1809–1865), sixteenth president of the United States

> "I object to people running down the future . . . [since] I am going to live all the rest of my life there, and I would like it to be a nice place, polished, bright, glistening, and glorious."
> —Charles Kettering (1876–1958), American twentieth-century engineer, inventor and founder of the Dayton Automotive Laboratory Company (DELCO)

> "The future ain't what it used to be."
> —Yogi Berra (1925–) New York Yankees' catcher and "king of malapropisms"

> "It is difficult to make predictions, especially about the future."
> —Niels Bohr (1885–1962), Danish physicist and colleague of Albert Einstein; also attributed to Enrico Fermi (1901–1954), American physicist and University of Chicago-based leader of the Manhattan Project, and Samuel Goldwyn (1879–1974), American movie mogul

> "We have to worry about the future."
> —Isaac Asimov (1920–1992), American science and science-fiction writer and futurist

> "If you do not think about the future, you won't have one."
> —John Galsworthy (1867–1933), English novelist and playwright; author of *The Forsyte Saga*

These future quotes make great beginnings for an overview talk you might develop if you are organizing a retreat or other meetings as a part of a strategic planning process, which we will consider next.

Planning at Its Best

For some, planning is a bore. For others, it is a source of cynicism. How often have you heard the remark "What? Another plan to put on the shelf to collect dust?" It's a remark that is too frequently true, especially in colleges and universities. Thus, when anticipating a planning effort, make sure that there is resolve for follow-through, which can make planning an invigorating and wholly worthwhile effort. The resolve is ensured if you are convinced—as most good academic administrators are—that planning is essential to success.

Planning—as regular meetings are —is one of those activities by which the performance of academic administrators is measured. Thus, it should be a part of any institution or unit you serve. We will consider long-range institution-wide planning in the next chapter. For now, we'll consider unit planning, which may range from larger academic affairs units to colleges or schools to organized academic or research units as considered in prior chapters. And, when planning is contemplated for such units, academic administrators most frequently use the term "strategic planning."

As a lifelong academic, I have long thought that "strategic planning" had a militaristic ring to it. Indeed, I poke fun at this notion when speaking about strategic planning by using—as an illustration—one of the many battle scenes depicted in the pop art works of Roy Lichtenstein (e.g., http://www.artchive.com/artchive/L/lichtenstein/lichtenstein_blam.html). During such presentations, I offer the suggestion that while the word "strategic" has military connotations, strategic planning has become so commonly used in the civilian sector of society that practically no professional can avoid understanding its use. So, let's consider the elements of strategic planning—beginning with vision.

Vision

Where are you headed? What will your unit look like when you get there? A vision is a statement—at best, a single sentence—developed to describe the destiny of an academic institution or some unit thereof. It sounds simple, but crafting a vision statement can take months, if not longer if you wish it to take hold among faculty members, students, and staff—if you wish it to achieve the status of a shared vision.

Given my experience at five major research universities, I have observed—firsthand—the difficulties large institutions have in crafting visions that are truly shared among faculty, students, and staff. Indeed, I have worked at institutions where I could have asked ten people about their institution's vision and received ten answers—many quite different from one another. Thus, I have appreciated my years at the University of Arkansas, where a clear and well-articulated vision was adopted in the early part of the twenty-first century and here it is: *The University of Arkansas is a nationally competitive, student-centered research university serving Arkansas and the world.*

Let's dissect this vision statement to find elements that have universal appeal. First, consider "nationally competitive." The university did not always think of itself in these terms. Competitive in football and basketball, yes, but in academics the claim was, for some, questionable. Thus, the "nationally competitive" claim was important to the institution's leadership who knew that academic prowess had to rival athletic strengths if the university was to achieve long-term respectability in academic circles.

Consider next "student-centered research university." The term "research university" speaks for itself, but it also suggests that the institution is of a size that is typical of research universities, which implies an impersonal atmosphere. Therefore "student-centered" was purposefully included to emphasize the special efforts of the institution to make it truly student-centered.

And, finally consider "serving Arkansas and the world." This says it well. It recognizes the support the institution receives from its home state. Likewise, the phrase denotes the importance that the university community places on giving back to its state, nation, and the world.

While the University of Arkansas may be considered to have successfully crafted an effective vision statement, elements of the latter could readily be used or adapted by many other institutions. For example, "nationally competitive" could easily be swapped with "nationally prominent" or "world class." "Student-centered" could be replaced by references to community orientation or other phraseology such as putting "students first." The phrase, "serving Arkansas and the world," could be supplanted by one with references to an alternative town, city, state, or nation. So, with these and other general elements in mind, one can craft a vision statement for academic institutions and units thereof. For example, one might imagine vision statements for units within a university with a vision such as the University of Arkansas's as follows:

- ■ The College of Health Sciences is a nationally competitive, student-centered research college serving the state and the world.
- ■ The College of Technology is one of the top fifty student-centered U.S. research colleges serving the state and the world.

Once a vision is crafted you will find people erroneously referring to it as a "mission statement." The two are clearly different. Let's remind ourselves how.

Mission

What do you do? How do you do it? These questions when answered properly help to define the mission of a college or university.

When tackling these questions, you may wish to consider the following characteristics:

- ■ Quality
- ■ Scope
- ■ Responsiveness to need
- ■ Effectiveness

Think about these characteristics and how they may play out in crafting mission statements for colleges and universities.

In most institutions, quality is the sine qua non of operations. Quality sets institutions apart and provides opportunities to develop a competitive edge.

Scope is also a critical consideration in defining mission, in part, because most professionals recognize that no institution can be all things to all people without sacrificing quality.

Responsiveness to need should be included in a mission statement because it helps in defining a niche. Addressing responsiveness to needs of prospective students, faculty, and staff also helps to define the economic, social, and cultural importance of a college or university.

Effectiveness or efficacy can be defined in terms of the quality of graduates' education and their success as well as the institution's impact on society.

Consider then, how these characteristics might be incorporated into mission statements for colleges and universities. For example, following is the mission statement of Middlebury College in Vermont:

The mission of Middlebury College is to educate students in the tradition of the liberal arts. Our academic program, co-curricular activities, and support services exist primarily to serve this purpose. Middlebury College is committed to excellence throughout its liberal arts curriculum: to balance in its academic offerings; to selective development of carefully chosen emerging strengths; and to maintaining conspicuous excellence in those areas of its traditional strengths such as language, literature, and an international perspective, including study abroad.

The following from the University of Michigan exemplifies a university's mission statement:

> The mission of the University of Michigan is to serve the people of Michigan and the world through preeminence in creating, communicating, preserving and applying knowledge, art, and academic values, and in developing leaders and citizens who will challenge the present and enrich the future.

As an example of a private sectarian university mission statement, consider the following from St. John's University in New York:

> As a university, we commit ourselves to academic excellence and the pursuit of wisdom which flows from free inquiry, religious values and human experience. We strive to preserve and enhance an atmosphere in which scholarly research, imaginative methodology, global awareness and an enthusiastic quest for truth serve as the basis of a vital teaching-learning process and the development of lifelong learning. Our core curriculum in the liberal arts and sciences aims to enrich lives as well as professions and serves to unify the undergraduate experience. Graduate and professional schools express our commitment to research, rigorous standards, and innovative application of knowledge.
>
> We aim not only to be excellent professionals with an ability to analyze and articulate clearly what is, but also to develop the ethical and aesthetic values to imagine and help realize what might be.

With an understanding of where you are going (vision) and the how and what you will doing to get there (mission), you now have the opportunity to consider the environment for growth and development. Commonly referred to as "environmental scanning," we'll consider this contextual element next.

Environmental Context

Strategic planners know that their future and effectiveness are not entirely in their hands. Indeed, the context for their operations will have a bearing on successes in achieving goals and objectives. The context for strategic planning is thus defined by institutional strengths and weaknesses as well as external opportunities and threats (these four factors are commonly referred to as the SWOT of strategic planning). Let's think a bit more about these factors.

The strengths of higher-education institutions can be defined in terms of the relevant quality and numbers of people, programs, and resources. Weaknesses can be assessed over the same range of factors. For all institutions, strengths may not necessarily be related to size. As noted above, successful colleges and universities know that there is power in being selective—in seeking excellence in a few areas rather than achieving mediocrity over a wider range of activities.

Opportunities and threats require a bit of prognostication and a broad understanding of the milieu of operations. Let's consider some relevant allusions to institutions used as examples in the mission section above.

Given its dedication to study abroad and education with an international perspective, what, for example, might Middlebury College officials do to help their students compete effectively for prominent international scholarships and fellowships? Considering the University of Michigan's dedication to "challenge the present and enrich the future," how might it best match this element of its mission with curricula offerings, including certificate programs? And, for St. John's University, how might it use continuing education programs to address its dedication to the "development of lifelong learning" among its graduates?

Posing such questions may assist discussions leading to the environmental scans that are critical to institutions. And, it should be obvious that the scans must be much more thorough than I have been in the few questions posed above. Indeed, the scans could include the development of benchmark data, which would consist of critical comparisons of a college's or university's characteristics with that of peers or competitors.

In many higher-education institutions, offices of institutional research can be enlisted in gathering data comparing the qualities of students (e.g., entering grade-point averages, high-school class rankings), faculty (e.g., percentages of faculty with doctorates), programs (e.g., student-faculty ratios, success of students in state-licensing examinations), and institutional performance measures (e.g., research funding, size of endowments) relative to sets of peers. The comparisons assist the elaboration of sets of strengths and weaknesses that inform discussions of opportunities and threats.

With carefully crafted environmental scans in place, academic administrators can engage faculty and staff in the shaping of sets of goals and objectives to support missions and assist in achieving visions. Let's now consider this next step in strategic planning.

Goals and Objectives

To realize a vision, to serve a mission, and to achieve success, institutions need goals and objectives. While occasionally used interchangeably, more often than not goals are considered as long term or what I like to think of as overarching end points whereas objectives relate to shorter-term results.

To exemplify the notions noted above, we can think of goals that might be drafted for a hypothetical liberal arts college:

I. Seek excellence in all programs.
II. Enhance diversity of faculty, students and staff.
III. Increase numbers of academic programs.
IV. Develop a mix of public and private funding to ensure infrastructure support and program viability.

Sample objectives corresponding to two of the college's goals might be as follows:

I. Seek excellence in all programs.
   1. Engage two to three nationally or internationally recognized scholars each year in a visiting-professor program.
   2. Institute a sabbatical program to enrich faculty development.
II. Enhance diversity of faculty, students, and staff.
   1. Develop a strategic investment fund to assist in the hiring of underrepresented faculty members.
   2. Institute a faculty-mentoring program.
   3. Develop and offer diversity workshops for all faculty and staff.

Establishing a set of goals and objectives completes a basic strategic plan, but questions may now be asked about implementation. Thus, implementation plans or related documents will often be developed to help the transition from planning to action.

During the crafting of implementation plans, consideration should be given to the meshing of planning with budgeting. Let's consider this topic next.

Meshing Planning and Budgeting

During one of my years of service to the University of Texas at Austin, students running for president and vice-president of the Student Governance Organization challenged the university with the following tongue-in-cheek admonition: "Why don't you remove the saying—'Ye shall know the truth and the truth shall make you free'—from the Texas Tower and replace it with 'Money talks.'" There are probably many faculty members at college and universities who would echo such a sentiment, especially with respect to academic budgeting. Thus, strategic planning and budgeting should both be considered when formulating priorities for funding.

Priorities are also key elements in budget reallocation efforts that are commonly observed in higher-education institutions. What better way to mesh priorities and budgeting than to have units—principally at the college and school levels—to consider the consequences of realigning funding from lower-priority programs and efforts to those designated higher-priority?

In universities I have served, reallocations were sometimes necessitated by budget cuts, but even in years of increased budgets, reallocation exercises conducted at the college level with presentations to executive councils or their equivalent (i.e., including leadership from university governance groups) went a long way in helping match funding to priorities and stated goals and objectives.

For deans and department chairs, no stronger signal can be sent to faculty, students, and staff than aligning budgets with college or department priorities. Thus, deans should work closely with their academic units in the preparation of budget proposals requested by central administrative officers.

In summary, strategic planning ought to be part of the modus operandi of colleges, schools, departments, and other academic units. Strategic planning should also guide budgeting operations of all academic units and programs. Unit strategic plans, however, should reflect long-range planning efforts and documents developed under the executive leadership of colleges and university. We'll consider such executive-led long-range planning in the next chapter.

CHAPTER 18

College- and University-wide Planning and Development

The State of North Carolina made a bold move in the 1960s, one watched across the nation, by investing in its research universities and creating Research Triangle Park. This was followed by a parallel effort in the late '90s to establish the centennial campus at North Carolina State University to provide services for emerging businesses and start-ups as RTP did for established high tech businesses. The dividends of these investments to the state, as well as the continued investment in public higher education, have been phenomenal. The North Carolina experience caused other states to make investments in their research universities.

—MARY ANNE FOX (1921–), chancellor,
University of California, San Diego

Institution-wide planning typically emanates from the executive leadership of a college or university. Because a variety of academic administrators are often asked to contribute, it is good to have a common understanding of the process and results of such planning. This chapter contains an overview of institutional planning and considers an example of such efforts from the perspective of a public research university. At the end, ideas are offered on how institutional planning may be integrated into institutional development, including fund-raising efforts.

Having a Vision

As noted in the previous chapter, crafting a vision—preferably a single sentence—is a primary objective of institution-wide planning. So it was for the University of Arkansas's flagship campus in Fayetteville, when new executive leadership came into office in the late nineties. During 1999–2000, a vision statement was adopted: *The University of Arkansas is a nationally competitive, student-centered research university serving Arkansas and the world.*

While the new vision statement began taking hold among faculty, students, and staff, developing common understanding was aided immensely by an institutional planning process, headed by a group known as the 2010 Commission. The idea for the commission and institution-wide planning was driven by the premise that while the vision and mission of the university may be clear to some groups within the institution, a series of questions addressing the understanding of those outside the university should be asked: :

- Is it understood by the people served by the university—especially among the students and state citizens at large?
- Do the state's citizens understand the benefits of a nationally competitive research university?
- Do they know how the state's future prosperity is inextricably linked to the success of the state's flagship institution?
- And if the above questions are valid, do they understand what it takes to build and sustain a research university that serves the state's needs?

These questions guided the formation of the Commission, which is considered next.

The 2010 Commission

Under the leadership of Chancellor John White, the 2010 Commission—a group of ninety-two business, government, and academic professionals and students—was appointed and charged with studying and presenting answers to the above questions and others deemed critical to the health of the university and the state. A prominent alumnus and business leader was chosen to chair the commission, while support for the commission's organizational efforts was placed in the hands of the university's provost, who served as the commission's executive secretary.

The commission's first charge was to prepare a report, *Making the Case: The Impact of the University of Arkansas on the Future of the State of Arkansas* (2001), which would become a primary communication vehicle to

- Demonstrate that the state's economic future demands a research university ranked among the nation's top fifty public institutions
- Delineate the university's role in driving the intellectual, economic, and cultural imperatives of the state
- Identify and assess the financial support that would be necessary for the university to reach its goals, based on wise stewardship of current resources

Crafting *Making the Case* involved not only meetings of the commission but also a series of campus-based focus groups, involving faculty, students, and staff, and organized to ensure that the university's efforts were recognized and that input into the process and substance of the report were welcomed. As the focus groups were conducted, a series of papers was written by the commission chair and executive secretary and the content of these papers—including understanding resulting from the focus-group sessions—ultimately became the major source of material for *Making the Case*. Below are the titles of five of the key papers in the series noted:

- "Advancing the State's Flagship University—Challenges Posed by Recent Higher Education Initiatives in Arkansas"
- "Making a Difference in Arkansas and the World—The Role of Higher Education in Society"
- "Arkansas Included—The Roles and Benefits of Research Universities"
- "Arkansas in Context—How Arkansas and the University of Arkansas Compare"
- "Closing the Gap—Making the Case for the University of Arkansas and Arkansas"

The papers (Rutledge and Smith, 2000) were published in the university's on-line journal *All Things Academic* and shared with commission members, and members of the university community and the public. Two of the papers were published in a local newspaper, at the request of its publisher.

Besides the papers—key to the development of the narrative sections of the report—the chancellor's proposals on benchmarking (i.e., against fifty-three of the leading public research universities in the nation) and a pledge to report annually any progress toward published goals captured the imagination and interest of business professionals, government, and civic leaders statewide. Indeed, the positive responses to the *Making the Case* report became part of a rationale for the commission members to recommend continuance of the commission's work through the decade of 2000–2010, thus giving new meaning to the "2010" in its title.

As of 2006, a total of three reports have been produced. Besides *Making the Case* in 2001, the commission produced *Picking up the Pace* in 2004 and *Gaining Ground* in 2005. The last two reports have been credited with helping to raise the stature of the university and assisting the adoption of a statewide funding formula that—for the first time in the institution's history—recognizes the unique mission of the university. Thus, planning turned into action, and the action favorably affected public support and funding of the university. What more could you ask?

Seriously, involvement in the work of the 2010 Commission made me a firm believer in institution-wide planning. But, the success of the commission's efforts has to be attributed in large measure to the highly effective benchmarking, goal setting, and annual reporting efforts instigated and encouraged by the university's chancellor. And, as noted in evidence published in *Picking Up the Pace*, the 2010 Commission effort has served as a model regionally and nationally for institution-wide planning—a model whose elements have been adopted by sister institutions including Louisiana State University, Texas A & M University, the University of Mississippi and the University of Texas at Austin, to name just a few.

Summarizing to this point, institution-wide planning—whether from the perspective of a college or university—can have a powerfully positive effect on common understanding of an institution's vision, mission, goals, and objectives. Inherent in this understanding is a grasp of the strengths, weaknesses, opportunities, and threats to the institution. An awareness of the strengths and opportunities—in particular—provides a vital source of ideas for university development, especially fund raising, as we will consider next.

Institutional Planning as a Guide to Fund Raising

Institutional planning is a powerful tool for clarifying a college's or university's vision, mission, goals, and objectives—all built on an understanding of the strengths, weaknesses, opportunities, and threats relevant to the institution's future. Institutional planning should also assist collegiate and university communities in shaping priorities for future development and herein lies the tie to fund raising.

Days are long gone when gifts and donations were made to institutions based primarily on some nebulous institutional affection or sentimental sense of support. Today, donors want to know precisely how their donated funds will impact the institution and, once donations are made, how the institution will be accountable. Thus, the preparation of proposals, contacts with prospective donors, and gift stewardship cry out for a strong planning base—one that comes with institutional planning of the caliber described for the 2010 Commission. Indeed, much of the background understanding of the institution and its potential successes—emanating from the work of the 2010 Commission and related college-based strategic planning efforts provided critical background for the completion of the University of Arkansas's one-billion-dollar Campaign for the Twenty-First Century (*Imagine, Inquire, Impart Report,* 2005).

The take-home messages for integrating institution-wide planning and development is this:

- ■ Think broadly in crafting a plan for and reporting on institutional planning, including prominent members of your state, national, or international constituencies.
- ■ Be sure to involve a broad cross section of the institution's community, including faculty members, students, and staff, to begin seeding ideas of the institution-wide efforts in the various units of the university or college.
- ■ Emphasize the disclosure of strengths and opportunities across the institution, again emphasizing how such efforts serve as a model for parallel subunits of the university or college.
- ■ Make sure that the university or college's vision is repeated, paraphrased, and emphasized in all institutional communications, including strategic plans of university or college units.
- ■ Use university- and college-wide planning reports and related documents as platforms for development proposals, especially those crafted for fund-raising efforts.
- ■ Finally, consider leading-edge thinking on integrating academic and fund-raising and development efforts as described by Gearhart (2006).

Summarizing this chapter, we have considered the impact of institution-wide planning on college and university advancement and development including fund-raising efforts. Through an institutional case study summary, a link was made between planning and success in academic development—broadly defined.

This chapter completes section III and a series of chapters containing guidance to various academic administrators and support staff. We now move on to section IV and a set of chapters on assessments and evaluations.

SECTION IV

Assessments and Evaluations

PREAMBLE

Just as goals and objectives are vital to academic unit and institutional planning, measuring progress toward such ends require assessment and evaluation. Assessments include internally initiated periodic college or departmental reviews as well as accreditations by regional associations (the entire university or college) or narrower discipline-based accreditations. We'll consider the role of academic administrators in such assessments in the first chapter of this section. The second chapter is devoted to evaluations of personnel, including the use of surveys to better understand constituent perceptions of leadership. So, let's move on to assessments, accreditations, and evaluations.

chapter 19

Assessments and Accreditation

Since 1895, when institutional accrediting agencies first appeared on the scene in U.S. higher education, people have been remarkably willing to trust their educational investments and futures to a unique and little-understood mechanism. Today, with new and unfamiliar educational providers appearing—including for-profit universities, distance-delivery colleges, higher-education chains, and transnational organizations— it is critical that both higher educators and the public appreciate what quality really means in education, and how accreditation can help to promote it.

—STEPHEN D. SPANGEHL (1943–), director,
Academic Quality Improvement Program,
North Central Association of Schools and Colleges

Making progress with action plans requires assessments—to determine achievement, to consider possible midcourse corrections or interventions, and to stay on track. Some assessments involve internal organizational structures, commitments, and follow-through. Other assessments, such as those connected with rating organizations (e.g., *U.S. News and World Report*) and accrediting agencies—both regional and discipline-based—require specifically directed personnel and efforts. Let's consider all of these efforts.

Internal Assessments

Regardless of your position within a college or university, assessments will be part of your administrative life. Programs, departments, and collegiate units are commonly assessed on a cycle of five to ten years. The actual assessment directives and their periodicity may be governed by state statute or policies within state higher-education agencies or the institutions themselves—for public institutions. Private institutions will typically have internal policies mandating assessments. Because of the ubiquitous nature of assessments, it is important for academic administrators from program directors to department chairs and deans to central academic administrative officers to know the who, what, when, why, and how often of internal assessment processes.

Frequently, colleges or universities establish assessment offices with staff to carry out assessment activities. It is important to know these personnel along with leading staff members in your institutional research office (or its equivalent) who are typically charged with the responsibility of gathering data that support assessment processes. Beyond purely internal data, your institutional research colleagues will also assist with collecting data for benchmarking efforts.

In our earlier discussions about planning, I mentioned benchmarking against peer institutions. The choice of peers is important, and the institutions selected should have scope and mission statements similar to that of the institution being assessed. For example, the peer group chosen for the University of Arkansas flagship campus in Fayetteville includes the public research universities in the Atlantic Coast Conference, the Big East (save Rutgers University because of budget reporting differences with the other institutions within the set), the Big Ten, the Big Twelve, the Pacific Athletic Conference, the Southeastern Conference, and two other institutions (i.e., Colorado State University and the University of Delaware) making a total of fifty-three peers (*Making the Case,* 2001). Other public research universities might choose a similar set or subset of this group or possibly establish a unique set of peers from among members of the National Association of State Universities and Land-Grant Colleges (NASULGC, 2006).

Public or private universities in the elite Association of American Universities (AAU, 2006) with its sixty-two (sixty U.S. and two Canadian) members might choose a set of peer institutions from among the AAU listing. Public urban research universities might consider institutions such as San Diego State University, the University of Colorado at Denver, the

University of Illinois at Chicago, the University of Pittsburgh, the University of Texas at Dallas, and Wayne State University, among others. For comprehensive (previously known as regional) universities and colleges— public or private—peers could be chosen from lists in the relevant categories used by *U.S. News and World Report* or from members of organizations such as the Association of American Colleges and Universities (AACU, 2006), the National Association of Independent Colleges and Universities (NAICU, 2006), or NASULGC. Again, it is important to match scope and mission statements of your institution and those of potential peers.

Sometimes state coordinating bodies try to dictate sets of peers for public research or comprehensive universities, and in these cases, it is important for academic administrators and chief executive officers of those institutions to seek input into the peer selection. Ideally, peers should include aspirant as well as average peers, but lawmakers or policymakers may choose lower-quality and more poorly funded peers than desirable— out of ignorance or possibly to lower the bar on resource expectations of state-based institutions.

Once peers are chosen, a set of benchmarks should be chosen for comparisons longitudinally. In the 2010 Commission work noted in chapter 18, the benchmarks chosen included academic reputation (from *U.S. News and World Report*), undergraduate acceptance rate, American College Testing (ACT) or ACT equivalent mid-range score, average high-school grade-point average (GPA) of entering freshmen, percent freshmen from upper decile in high school, freshman retention rate, six-year graduation rate, student-to-faculty ratio, percent undergraduate classes under twenty students, percent undergraduate classes with more than fifty students, and state appropriations per student, among others. Additional benchmarks could include measures related to research funding and scholarly productivity, and now with the services of companies such as Academic Analytics (http://academicanalytics.net/), measures of faculty scholarly productivity across institutions are more feasible.

At the University of Arkansas, administrators (Smith and Pederson, 2001) have also conducted assessments and evaluations based on student semester credit hours (SSCH) per full-time equivalent (FTE) tenure track (TT) faculty member; external funds per FTE TT faculty member; cost per SSCH based on individual program budgets; undergraduate, graduate, or professional degree production; and total undergraduate/graduate or professional students per FTE TT faculty member, using data from the Delaware Study (2006; Middaugh, 2003), which uses data from the National Center for Education Statistics (2006) and provides tracking of performances of fifty-three research and comprehensive universities in thirty-one states and the District of Columbia. While the comparison data and subsequent analyses had some continuing merit in budgeting efforts, the initial study was received with considerable criticism when it was shared with departmental personnel across the institution because of a lack of specific measures of academic quality.

Besides university-based benchmarking, college- or department-wide benchmarking may be pursued through information obtained from sources noted above, in addition to data that can be accessed through an institutional research office. A college of engineering wishing to enter the ranks of the top fifty public colleges in America could, for example, craft a planning and benchmarking effort to assess progress towards its goal through resources noted earlier along with those available—in the case of engineering—from ABET (2006), which describes itself as "a federation of twenty-eight professional and technical societies representing the fields of applied science, computing, engineering, and technology."

The reference to ABET, and by implication accrediting agencies, offers a good segue to the broader topic of accreditation, which we'll consider next.

Accreditation and Assessments

Accreditation adds value to degree programs and in some professional areas (e.g., health professions, social work) is obligatory for graduates to sit for state licensing examinations. There was a time, however, when accrediting bodies and the processes they represent were the bane of central administrators. In the words of one colleague, some years ago, "They come through here, determine the program is under-funded and emerge during the exit interview demanding additional resources for the program under review." Fortunately, this is no longer the case. Rather, a philosophy pervasive currently among accrediting agencies can be stated as, "It is not our job to dictate funding but to assess how well a unit is doing given its funding and other resources."

Besides shifting from a funding fixation, accrediting agencies have—in recent years—become much more oriented to issues of diversity and learning outcomes (Ratcliff, et al., 2001; Spangehl, 2004). And, these realities are apparent whether we refer to regional accrediting bodies such as the Higher Learning Commission of the North Central Association of Colleges and Schools or any number of discipline-based accrediting agencies such as those of the American Psychological Association. Accordingly, accreditation may serve as an opportunity for objective assessment of programs and may supplant the need for internal evaluations, although coordination of internally and externally driven assessments represents a valuable way of insuring assessments across an entire institution.

In general, assessment may be thought of as a four-step process: 1) self-study, 2) objective evaluation including determinations of strengths and weaknesses and recommendations for changes, 3) responses by administrators and faculty of the units assessed, and 4) final accord—preferably in writing—for future action among unit personnel, their supervisory individuals, and the accrediting agency (where relevant). Reaching accord, documenting understandings, and following up with planning, implementation, and future assessments represent powerful factors for growth and development.

In summary, assessments—including those driven entirely from within the institutions—provide effective mechanisms for planning, evaluations, and commitments for validation and change within an institution. The effectiveness of these efforts are enhanced by benchmarking against a well-thought-out group of peers. And, while the evaluation of individual personnel—particularly faculty members and academic administrators is implicit in assessments, more formal one-on-one evaluations of these academic professionals require a different set of strategies and efforts as will be considered in the next chapter.

20

Evaluations of Personnel

Humankind cannot bear very much reality.
                    —T. S. ELIOT (1888–1965), American critic,
                                    essayist, poet, and playwright

People are the heart of each and every academic program. During my long academic life, I have never ceased to be impressed how important capable, talented, and creative people are to the initiation, development, and growth of academic programs and, of course, in instructing, mentoring, and inspiring students. Finding and nurturing such gifted and necessary souls requires evaluations.

In this chapter, we will consider the role of personnel evaluations in the hiring and periodic assessments of academics from administrative staff to directors, chairs, and deans. I will offer suggestions for evaluative procedures that supervisors can adopt along with suggestions for augmenting evaluations through surveys and other information-gathering processes. So, let's get started with hiring.

They Hired Who?

If you have been in academic administration for some time, you may relate to experiences of having hired or being directly involved in the hiring of hundreds of professionals—both from within and beyond home institutions. With such an experience base, you have also undoubtedly witnessed the hiring away of personnel from your institution—for posts near and far. Sometimes, you hear of these transitions after the fact and you may think, "They hired who?" because of what seems to be an inappropriate fit. You may also wonder—if you had been close administratively to the candidate, "Why didn't the hiring institution ask me about this person?"

Now, the above musings may seem arrogant, but they are not meant to be so. Rather, the scenarios noted are intended to make the point of how important evaluations are in the hiring of academic professionals—throughout the chain of command. Somewhat paradoxically, however, evaluation has become more complex in the United States in recent years because of challenges to confidentiality and an upsurge in litigation. If you have been involved in tenure denials, for example, you know how many of these decisions are tested through court proceedings or the threats thereof. But, all of this complexity reinforces the need for careful evaluations in hiring processes.

Hiring from within an institution has an advantage in that many people close to a candidate can be tapped for evaluations and recommendations. And, many of these evaluators will have seen the prospective candidate under stressful situations, thus providing a fairly complete picture of how the candidate might perform under challenging conditions.

In contrast to internal hires, recruiting candidates from other institutions, organizations, or firms requires scrupulous attention to evaluations and evaluators. It should almost go without saying that the evaluations should also include the verification of credentials because of high-profile examples, in recent years, of academic administrators being hired with bogus and misrepresented credentials. With the credentialing in hand, evaluations continue by seeking assessments from recommended references, other former supervisors, and colleagues.

Standard letters of recommendation have a role in personnel evaluations, but they are not enough to complete an evaluative process. Indeed, because of liberal freedom of information and disclosure statutes in various places in the United States, evaluators have become circumspect about comments included in "official" letters of recommendation. Thus, it is wise to follow up by telephone, avoiding e-mail that can be subpoenaed in possible future court actions. But, don't stop with the candidate's list of references. Once you have received permission from the candidate to make calls more widely, begin with selected individuals at the candidate's present or former place of employment. When talking with such individuals, seek names of people who know the candidate and particularly persons who may now be retired. I have found retired individuals to be invaluable sources of information primarily because they no longer have to fear any type of retaliation for their honesty.

The thoroughness recommended above does not come from pessimism or any mean spiritedness but from experiences I have had wherein references were not checked as carefully as called for and disasters resulted. I have also "dodged many a bullet" and avoided the hiring of truly problematic individuals through persistent telephonic assessments, as alluded to above.

Fortunately, the good people of our world outnumber the bad, and we all have opportunities to hire many fine individuals into myriad positions in the academy. Once on board, however, you will need to ensure top-flight performance by meaningful and effective periodic evaluations, as will be considered next.

Yearly Reviews

I have worked in academic settings where annual reviews—including one-on-one meetings with personnel—were greeted with comments such as, "I have never been reviewed like this before!" How sad. And how unfortunate— to think that personnel would not have received the kind of feedback that would have been helpful in professional development. But, let's step back. Evaluations don't begin with one-on-one meetings. Rather, one-on-one meetings should represent the penultimate step in an evaluation process that we will consider next.

There are clues to bases for evaluations in chapters 13–17. You will recall that in chapters 13–16 we defined roles and responsibilities for a range of academic administrative types from deans to chairs and heads to directors to administrative support professions. For example, we considered a body of literature that suggested roles for chairs in managing, leading, developing faculty, and pursuing personal scholarship. This set of responsibilities, and others that are delineated for additional types of academic administrative professionals, frame-out sets of expectations that are further shaped by the vision, mission, and goals of the academic unit served, as noted in chapter 17.

With the above thoughts in mind, we might consider a template for an annual-review self-evaluation document as follows:

Annual Evaluation
Name of Person Evaluated
College or University of _____
Yearly Period: _____

Document Completion Date: _____
Date of Last Review: _____

Preamble Statement

This self-evaluation is composed of a short narrative and lists of goals and accomplishments for the *(office or unit)* for the period of _____. I also offer a set of objectives for the next yearly review period. Appended is documentation on presentations, publications, national and regional service, and honors during the past year. I have also appended the results of a survey conducted by _____ with the following constituents: _____.

My goals for *(the office or unit)* have been to mesh the mission and efforts of my unit with the overarching goals of the *(larger unit[*(e.g., *college] or university)*, namely: 1) _____; 2) _____; 3) _____ and the goals and objectives contained in the unit's strategic plan, as articulated during the prior annual review.

Objectives for Next Year

Re the Unit's Goal Number One:
Re the Unit's Goal Number Two:
    Etc.

Accomplishments During the Past Year

Re the Unit's Goal Number One:
Re the Unit's Goal Number Two:
    Etc.

Appendix

Name of Person Evaluated
Presentations, Publications, National and Regional Service, and Honors
Yearly Period _____

As noted in the annual-review template, the self-evaluation can and probably should be augmented by a survey of constituents served. In this regard, I have found the service provided by the IDEA (Individual Development and Educational Assessment) Center (2006) at Kansas State University ("Feedback for Administrators") to be very useful in assessing leadership strengths and weaknesses. The fact that this survey is conducted completely objectively and independently of units offers special benefits.

With the self-evaluation and survey results in hand, you can have a meaningful yearly evaluation with all of your direct reports. During the penultimate one-on-one meeting, be sure to highlight noteworthy accomplishments, of both the unit and the individual evaluated. Also, review the survey results and seek agreement on areas where improvement might be in order. End with an understanding of where the individual is in his or her career plans and how the current review dovetails with other cyclical (e.g., five-year) reviews. Follow-up with documentation of the meeting and the review in an annual appraisal memorandum to the person evaluated. In such memoranda, I like to include the following types of language:

> I have continued to appreciate your leadership of the *(unit)* during *(period of review)*.
>
> Developments in the *unit* that I thought most notable included
>
> _____.
>
> I appreciate and encourage your pursuit of the *(unit's)* goals, including your commitment to *(specific goals or objectives)*. I know from our conversations, that your efforts will emphasize *(priority goals and objectives)*. Also, I continue to appreciate your personal dedication to teaching and scholarship.
>
> Finally, I valued having the opportunity to review the IDEA Feedback for Administrators survey. The results suggest that your constituents appreciate your _____. The results also suggest that you should consider improvements in the areas of _____, as we discussed during our one-on-one meeting. I look forward to our periodic meetings during the following year and additional opportunities to learn about progress towards your unit's goals, as well as action you are taking to continuously enhance service to your unit.
>
> Again, I want you to know that I have valued your dedication to your unit. I am pleased and honored to work with you as a colleague and friend.

The tone of the yearly evaluation should be one of understanding and helpfulness. One should avoid sounding overly negative or pessimistic unless there have been truly serious setbacks in the unit. In my experience, an emphasis on the negative can have truly devastating effects on individuals— much more than many supervisors would like to recognize. This philosophical bent has been guided by T. S. Eliot's admonition offered earlier: "Humankind cannot bear very much reality." Having made this point with great conviction, however, I must say I have faced situations where personnel had to be asked to step down from administrative posts—a decision based typically on objective reviews of multiyear periods of service. Let's consider these multiyear reviews in the context of a five-year review.

Looking across a Half Decade

It is common in academic institutions to consider multiyear reviews. Typically, these come after five-year periods, and it is useful to consider these more formidable reviews separate from yearly reviews. Although, it should be acknowledged that yearly reviews become the building blocks of reviews of lengthier service, as will be noted below.

At many higher-education institutions, a five-year review of deans and other administrators is common practice. The process for the review varies somewhat from institution to institution, even at the few places where I have worked, but outlined below is a process (University of Arkansas Academic Policy Series, 2005) that I have administered for several deans of schools and colleges—a process that would work well for any academic administrator:

- The review is typically administered every five years but may be instituted at any time deemed necessary. The take-home message being that the academic officer serves at the pleasure of her or his supervisor and may be asked to step down at any time.
- The chief academic office and chief executive officer confer on the wisdom of possibly reappointing (e.g., for another five years) the dean or certain other academic officers. With the concurrence and agreement of the dean in question, a review process may commence.
- The plan for the review may take one of three courses: 1) limited review by the chief academic officer, principally involving key constituent groups, 2) a formal process noted below, or 3) initial set of inquiries by the chief academic officer followed by a more formal process.
- A review committee is appointed, consisting typically of a dean or equivalent from another unit as chair and having representation for faculty, student, and staff, including at least one department chair or equivalent.
- The formal review commences with the following components: 1) a formal charge by the chief academic officer, 2) a request for a written self-evaluation by the academic officer reviewed, including the officer's assessment of the unit's strategic plan and progress towards goals and objectives during the review period, and a list of individuals the academic officer believes are familiar with his or her work, 3) a sharing of the self-evaluation and unit yearly reports with the review committee.
- The review committee is charged with meeting with constituent groups to solicit views on the academic officer's performance and accomplishments or setbacks during the review period. The work

may be augmented by information obtained through surveys of groups within and outside of the institution.

■ Given a reasonable period of time (e.g., three months), the review committee is directed to prepare a report containing their assessments and recommendations relative to 1) administrative and programmatic accomplishments deemed important during the review period, 2) significant challenges for the unit and those that require special attention, 3) recommendations relative to the academic officer's administrative style, policies, and procedures that might better serve the unit.

A report of chief academic officer's work or that of the formal review committee becomes the basis for recommendations to the chief executive officer when appropriate. A reappointment decision will be followed by discussions between the chief academic officer and the academic officer under review about conditions and followed up with a reappointment letter.

A decision not to reappoint a dean or other academic officer will typically be followed by angst-filled conversations among the chief academic and chief executive officers. A final decision should be based on a fair balancing of the academic officer's strengths and weaknesses and possible future productive roles for the individual in the institution.

In summary, we have considered the importance of evaluations during hiring processes and follow-up single and multiyear reviews. Some specific ideas have been offered on processes for such reviews and the heightened sense of humanity recommended to all who conduct reviews.

This chapter brings section IV to a close. We now move on to the final section and a set of chapters on policies and partnerships.

SECTION V

Policies and Partnerships

PREAMBLE

Policies provide operational principles and procedures not only for activities within institutions but also for dealings with the outside world and—in our time—supporting partnerships that are vital for institutions to serve the nation and the world. Academic administrators at all levels must understand and articulate institutional policies. Some of us may even contribute to the crafting of institution-wide policies. Thus, insight on the bases for and functions of policies—particularly those guiding ethical behavior of members of the academy—is highly useful.

This section begins with an overview of ethics-based policies in higher education, which is coupled with a chapter on the nettlesome area of conflicts of interest and commitment. The section continues with chapters on partnerships with a range of agencies from other academic institutions to governmental and nongovernmental organizations to businesses and corporations—near and far. The section, and the book ends, with some thoughts on a subject that "everybody talks about, but nobody does anything about"—the weather—and policies and procedures for dealing with inclement atmospheric behavior. So let's go on—first considering ethics-based policies.

Survey of Ethics-Based Policies in Higher Education

Wonk if you love policy.
  —bumper sticker spotted in the Washington, D.C.
  area during the Clinton administration (1992–2000)

In the summer of 2005, I was asked to organize a higher-education graduate seminar titled "Ethics Across the Public Higher-Education Landscape." It occurred to me during the preparation of that presentation that many academic administrators might appreciate a "view across the ethics-based policy landscape." Thus, this chapter was born with the caveat that a separate and more extensive treatment would also be needed for the nettlesome area of conflict of interest and commitment. The latter topic has been saved primarily for the next chapter. But, let's get on with our policy tour, beginning with a general framework for ethical obligations and policy development.

Ethical Standards and Obligations in Higher Education

Reading the title of this chapter, the cynic might quip, "There aren't any!" But, the overwhelming majority of academic administrators I have known understood and respected the covenants of fairness, honesty, justice, fiduciary responsibility, and public trust that undergird our institutions' daily operations and actions. Our colleagues also know and recognize that if public or institutional trust is abused, governmental agencies will assume the responsibility of dictating our policies. Indeed, those of us who have been around for decades remember abuses that led to federal statutes or regulations related to animal and human research, employment discrimination, student privacy, and misconduct in research, to name just a few.

Academic administrators who serve public institutions also understand obligations to state and municipal authorities. Thus, the development, implementation, and enforcement of college or university policies are time-consuming but necessary features of all academic administrators' professional lives.

Developing policies occurs at different levels of an institution or institutional system. For colleges or universities—whether or not they are members of a system of higher education—policy approvals are the responsibility of the governing board—be they referred to as curators, governors, regents, trustees, or the equivalent. For those institutions that are members of a university system, system-wide policies take precedent over institutionally specific policies in a manner parallel to the functioning of federal versus state statutes. Accordingly, when crafting policies specific to a given unit of university system, one must take care not to trump or contradict policies of the broader authority.

In my experience, university general counsel professionals are essential players in policy-making efforts. But, it is also important to take into account input from faculty governance groups. And, while the college or university governing boards have the final say, seeking accord among institutional constituents goes a long way in ultimately effecting compliance with implemented policies.

In chapter 16 we considered the role of a chief research officer in enforcing policies related to research and particularly those research-related policies emanating from federal statutes (e.g., misconduct in research). Thus, the chief research officer should have a leading role in the development of relevant policies, seeking reviews through appropriate faculty senate or assembly committees. In the end, however, policy adoption and enforcement becomes the primary purview of the central administration, as sanctioned by an institutional governing board.

Our policy tour now continues with specific ethics-based policy matters. To begin, we'll consider federally mandated privacy policies that have a significant impact on students and their lives in our institutions.

Family Rights and Privacy Act

Emanating from the Privacy Act of 1974, the Family Rights and Privacy Act (FERPA), assures parental access to school records for students under the age of eighteen. When students reach eighteen, they are entitled to block access to their records by parents so long as the students are financially independent. Thus, unless prohibited by institutional policy, adult students may accord access to their records by a parent or parents through a signed waiver. Alternatively, if it can be proven by a parent or parents that their progeny are financially dependent—typically by sharing a copy of a most recent federal income-tax filing—the parent or parents are entitled to access to records of students who are eighteen years old or older. In my experience, the last FERPA element is neither well known nor well understood in many institutions.

Besides the access options noted above, an institution may—without specific permission—release specific records (*Family Rights and Privacy Act, 2005*) to

- University or college officials who have a legitimate educational need to know
- Colleges or universities to which a student may be transferring
- Institutional officials or officials sanctioned to conduct accrediting, auditing, evaluation or administrative reviews, and procedural modifications (e.g., installation of new student information systems)
- Officials who are assisting students with financial aid
- Officials charged with assisting in cases of health and safety emergencies
- State or local juvenile justice system officials as mandated under specific state statutes

Under FERPA institutions "may disclose, without consent, 'directory' information such as a student's name, address, telephone number, date and place of birth, honors and awards, and dates of attendance. However, schools must tell parents and eligible students about directory information and allow parents and eligible students a reasonable amount of time to request that the school not disclose directory information about them."

In most colleges and universities, the registrar or equivalent has the responsibility for compliance with FERPA regulations and FERPA–related institutional policies and procedures.

Let's now move on to another critical student-centered policy matter involving students with disabilities.

Americans with Disabilities Act

Passed by the U.S. Congress in 1990, the Americans with Disabilities Act (ADA)—under Title II specifically—affirms rights to educational access and reasonable accommodations for students with disabilities. The ADA builds on Section 504 of the Rehabilitation Act of 1973 and collectively, the two pieces of legislation are designed to prevent discrimination in public accommodations provided by entities receiving federal funding (Grossman, 2001). In higher education, the ADA and its antecedent legislation guarantee equal access to educational information and reasonable accommodations to students possessing certifiable disabilities.

As noted by Grossman (2001), accommodations are indeed subject to measures of reasonableness, and students benefiting from the ADA must meet the "essential" (e.g., course requirements), "academic" (e.g., grade-point average), and "technical" (e.g., physical dexterity necessary to perform surgery) requirements of academic programs. Relative to academic accommodations for students, most institutions have offices or centers staffed with professionals who are conversant with ADA provisions, and these staff members have the background, skills, and experience to assess students needs and make recommendations on reasonable accommodations. For example, the director of the Center for Students with Disabilities at the University of Arkansas, Anne Jannarone (2006), directed me to a web-based resource maintained at the University of Washington—called the "The Faculty Room" (2006)—that contains a wealth of information on services for disabled students, including the development and delivery of reasonable accommodations. Policies regulating such efforts should offer examples of "reasonable accommodations" and procedures for appeals of judgments thereof.

There are many other federally mandated policies that impact the delivery of services to students, but the ones noted thus far are probably of greatest interest to academic administrators. We now move on to other significant compliance related policy areas that principally impact faculty, staff, and students who conduct research.

Human-Subjects Research

Few problems confronting academic administrators present any greater challenges than violations of policies pertaining to the use of human subjects in research. Thus, it behooves academic administrators to be conversant with the background and administration of relevant policies.

Federal regulations for human-subjects research (Code of Federal Regulations, U.S. Department of Health and Human Services, 2005a) are applicable only to federally sponsored research. Under the "principle of preemption," states, municipalities, and other bodies may not pass laws that lessen the impact of federal statutes. State legislative bodies and colleges or universities through institutional policy may, however, augment federal laws with their own policies. Indeed, many institutions apply federal regulations uniformly to research, regardless of sources of funding.

Questions about human-subjects regulations or the relevant Institutional General Assurance (IGA) can be directed to the staff of the office of research and sponsored programs or equivalent or to the chairperson of a university's Institutional Review Board (IRB) (see below). The Institutional General Assurance commits an institution to policy and procedures to ensure that subjects do not engage in research without being properly informed.

Informed consent involves the following characteristics:

1. Information: Subjects are given information on procedures, possible benefits, risks, and the qualifications of investigators before making judgments about participation.
2. Understanding: Investigators take measures to ensure that subjects understand the consequences of participation in the research.
3. Voluntariness: Subjects are given opportunities to contemplate their decision to participate, and they give consent without coercion and with the understanding that they may withdraw at any time.

The informed consent procedure must be carefully designed and administered; its completion is documented by a consent form. The consent form, therefore, is principally a legal instrument designed to protect the investigator and the institution.

Certain types of research are considered innocuous enough to permit an exempted or IRB–sanctioned expedited review. These categories of research include

1. Research conducted in established or commonly accepted educational settings and research that involves normal educational practices
2. Research involving the use of educational tests (cognitive, diagnostic, aptitude, achievement) if information taken from these sources is recorded so that subjects cannot be identified

3. Research involving survey or interview procedures, except where all of the following conditions exist:
   a. Responses are recorded so that human subjects can be identified, directly or through identifiers linked to the subjects
   b. The subject's responses, if they become known outside the research, could place the subject at risk of criminal or civil liability or be damaging to the subject's financial standing
   c. The research deals with sensitive aspects of the subject's own behavior
4. Research involving the observation (including observation of participants) of public behavior, except where all of the following conditions exist:
   a. Observations are recorded so that the human subjects can be identified
   b. The observations recorded about the individual, if they became known outside of the research, could place the subject at risk
   c. The research deals with sensitive aspects of the subject's own behavior
5. Research involving the collection or study of existing data, documents, records, pathological specimens, or diagnostic specimens, if these sources are publicly available or if the information is recorded so that subjects cannot be identified.

The principle of preemption applies to the expedited reviews, and it should be determined whether a university's IGA prescribes stricter rules. Whether exempted, expedited, or regular IRB–reviewed research is conducted, processes and standards should be in place to ensure that subjects are as informed as possible.

Institutional Review Boards. Society recognizes the importance of human-subjects research. It also strives to protect the powerless. Subjects enlisted in studies are generally naive about the research process. Their participation may be the first activity of its type in their lives. These individuals deserve the protection of informed consent and peer review. The peer-review process is accomplished through an IRB.

An IRB is a committee appointed by a college or university chief executive officer, but oversight of the committee's actions is typically delegated through the chief academic officer to the chief research officer or equivalent. The IRB has the following makeup (Code of Federal Regulations, U.S. Department of Health and Human Services, 2005):

- At least five members of varying backgrounds and expertise
- Neither all men nor women and a diverse membership based on race, ethnicity, professional identities, and sensitivity to community norms
- At least one member each from scientific and nonscientific areas (e.g., law, ethics, or theology)
- At least one member who is not affiliated with the institution or is not a member of a family of an employee of the institution

The IRB's chief responsibility is to decide whether research projects place subjects at risk, and if so

- Will the risks be outweighed by the benefits to the subject and the knowledge to be gained from the study?
- Will the rights and welfare of subjects be adequately protected?
- Will ethically appropriate and legally effective informed consent be secured from subjects?

Some institutions have a two-tiered review system. This means that proposals are normally reviewed at the departmental level before being considered by the IRB. Alternatively, certain low-risk studies may call for review and approval by only one or two members of the IRB (so-called expedited review). One additional option occurs with proposals for other low-risk (exempt) research that may only require review at the departmental level.

One further note. When conducting administrative surveys that may lead to publishable data and data-related conclusions (e.g., diversity climate surveys), it is best to seek IRB review and approval of the efforts. Indeed, the principle of erring on the cautious side is clearly apropos regarding human-subjects research. This advice is also apropos for animal research, which will be considered next.

Animal Research

After World War II, biomedical research increased markedly in the United States, however, not without some abuses by researchers and animal suppliers. Coincident animal-rights activities and a heightened awareness of animal-welfare issues by the public elicited responses from the federal government. A series of surveys of animal research performed by the National Institutes of Health in the sixties led to the passage of the

Animal Welfare Act of 1966 (and amendments in 1970, 1976, and 1985) and publication of a guide for laboratory care, *Guide for the Care and Use of Laboratory Animals* (1996). The *Guide* plus regulations of the Animal and Plant Health Inspection Service (APHIS) of the United States Department of Agriculture (Code of Federal Regulations, U.S. Department of Agriculture, 1996), contain minimum requirements for the handling, maintenance, and transportation of live vertebrate animals.

Institutions receiving NIH funds for research with animals must submit an assurance document to the Office of Laboratory Animal Welfare (National Institutes of Health, 2005) committing these institutions to the principles in the *Guide for the Care and Use of Laboratory Animals*. The same institutions must also submit to yearly inspections of facilities by APHIS professionals.

A college or university's animal assurance requires establishment of an Institutional Animal Care and Use Committee (IACUC, pronounced "I, a cook") to approve and review animal research activities on campus. The IACUC is often appointed by the college's or university's chief executive officer, but oversight of the committee's actions is typically delegated through the chief academic officer to the chief research officer or equivalent. IACUCs must have at least five members whose background and experience is relevant to the committee's responsibilities. At least one member of the committee must be a veterinarian who is likely to be responsible for animal care at the institution (i.e., campus veterinarian). The committee must also have at least one nonscientist member (e.g., ethicist, lawyer) and a member who is unaffiliated with the institution and who is not an immediate family member of an institutional employee. Akin to human-subjects research regulations, animal-research guidelines can be strengthened by state or local statutes and by university policies.

The guiding principles of animal research are as follows:

Personnel
1. Experiments with live, vertebrate animals and tissues from living animals must be conducted under the supervision of qualified biological, behavioral, and medical scientists.
2. Housing, care, and feeding of experimental animals must be supervised by a qualified veterinarian.

Research
1. Research must be designed to yield results for the good of society. Experiments must not be random or unnecessary.

2. Experiments should be based on knowledge of diseases or problems under study with anticipated results that justify their performance.

3. Mathematical models and in vitro biological systems should be used whenever possible to reduce the numbers of animals needed.

4. All unnecessary suffering and injury to animals must be avoided during experimentation.

5. Investigators must terminate experiments when it is believed that continuation may result in unnecessary suffering and injury to animals.

6. If experiments are likely to cause greater discomfort than that attending anesthetization, animals must be treated appropriately with an analgesic. The only exception to this is cases where drug treatment defeats the purpose of the experiment and data cannot be obtained by any other humane procedure. Such experiments must be scrupulously supervised by qualified senior scientists.

7. Postexperimental care of animals must minimize discomfort and consequences of any disability resulting from the experiment, in accordance with acceptable veterinary practice.

8. Euthanasia must be accomplished in a humane manner using acceptable practices and insuring immediate death. No animal should be disposed of until death is certain.

Facilities and Transportation

1. Standards for construction and use of housing, service, and surgical facilities should meet those described in the *Guide for the Care and Use of Laboratory Animals* (1996).

2. Transportation of animals must meet standards and regulations intended to reduce discomfort, stress, and spread of disease. All animals received for experimental purposes must be promptly uncrated and placed in permanent facilities.

Beyond the ethical issues associated with the protection of animals in research, few issues are as emotionally and politically charged. But, research and policies pertaining to the use of biohazards and radioactive and toxic materials come in collectively as a close second. We'll continue this survey then with these topic areas—beginning with biohazards.

Biohazards

Potential or real biohazards include recombinant DNA molecules, etiologic agents (e.g., viruses, bacteria, fungi, parasitic agents), oncogenic viruses, and chemicals that are radioactive or potentially toxic (including carcinogenicity) to animals and humans. A variety of federal guidelines or standards exist for the use and disposal of these agents, including the Laboratory Registration and Select Agents Transfer Tracking Program, which was established through the Antiterrorism and Effective Death Penalty Act of 1996 and is regulated through the Centers for Disease Control and Prevention (Code of Federal Regulations, Department of Health and Human Services, 1996). We'll consider regulations and policies pertaining to these agents in this and one other section that follows.

RECOMBINANT DNA MOLECULES

The initial significant research efforts with recombinant DNA material occurred in the early seventies. As noted by Fredrickson (1979), the first few years of recombinant DNA research were marked by controversy. The potential hazards of inserting foreign genetic material into common gut bacteria such as *Escherichia coli* were either overstated or misunderstood. Progress in this field of research has given scientists and federal officials more realistic perspectives that have been used to prepare the most recently adopted guidelines (National Institutes of Health, 2002).

The guidelines recommend the formation of an Institutional Biosafety Committee (IBC), which reviews and approves the construction and handling of recombinant DNA molecules and microorganisms (including viruses) containing recombinant DNA molecules. In the context of the guidelines, recombinant DNA molecules are 1) molecules constructed outside living cells by joining natural or synthetic DNA segments to DNA molecules which are subsequently replicated in a living cell or 2) DNA molecules replicated as a result of the steps in 1. If a synthetic DNA segment is not expressed in vivo yielding a biologically active polynucleotide or polypeptide, then it is exempt from the guidelines.

Akin to the IRB and IACUC, the IBC is typically appointed by the institution's chief executive officer, but oversight of the committee's actions is delegated through the chief academic officer to the chief research officer or equivalent of the college or university. The IBC consists of no fewer than five members who collectively have expertise in recombinant DNA technology. They must also be capable of assessing the safety of recombinant DNA research and the risks of this research to public health and the environment. At least two members of the IBC must not be affiliated with the university and should represent public health and environmental interests of the surrounding community. The IBC's responsibility in recombinant DNA research is to evaluate proposals for potential hazards and to ensure that suitable precautions are adopted. And, on many campuses, the IBC will be responsible for all biohazards, as will be noted below, not just those associated with recombinant DNA molecules.

MICROBIOLOGICAL HAZARDS

Etiologic agents and oncogenic viruses are two biohazards that require special handling. Under the federal Laboratory Registration and Select Agents Transfer Tracking Program (Code of Federal Regulations, Department of Health and Human Services, 1996) and typical institutional policies, the use of such agents in teaching and research requires prior approval of the IBC. Important components of biohazards policies include monitoring of relevant research efforts including yearly reviews among researchers and supervisors.

Beyond biohazards, academic administrators should be aware of policies pertaining to the use of radiation and radioactive materials, toxic chemicals, and dangerous drugs in teaching and research. Let's consider briefly these areas next.

Radiation Hazards, Toxic Chemicals, and Dangerous Drugs

The use of devices emitting ionizing radiation or radioactive materials, toxic chemicals (including carcinogens), and dangerous drugs in teaching and research are regulated through policies enforced by safety officers who typically report through the chief research officer and chief academic officer or chief administrative officer. Let's consider each domain separately.

RADIATION HAZARDS

Institutional radiation safety policies and programs emanate from laws and regulations of the U.S. Nuclear Regulatory Commission (2005), the U.S. Environmental Protection Agency (2005), and the U.S. Department of Homeland Security (2005) along with individual state departments of health and environmental quality (or their equivalents). Because of the highly technical nature of radiation hazards, academic administrators should advocate for the highest credentialing (i.e., certification in health physics) and competence in a college or university radiation safety officer. The radiation safety officer must interact effectively with a radiation safety committee, which is appointed analogously to the IRB, IACUC, and IBC.

The chief research officer should work closely with the radiation safety officer and the radiation safety committee to craft policies for the use of radiation devices and the use and disposal of radioactive materials. In all of this policy development and related implementation, the radiation safety officer must coordinate his or her responsibilities with college or university environmental-safety officers, and work from an integrated understanding of state and federal regulations including relevant principles of preemption. Specifically, when dealing with issues of mixed radioactive and chemical wastes, the typical preemptory authority of health departments over those devoted to environmental quality should be clearly recognized and acknowledged in clean-up efforts. I have observed misunderstandings of the principles of preemption to the detriment of higher-education institutions, including fines and adverse publicity.

TOXIC CHEMICALS

Institutional toxic-chemical policies and programs emanate from laws and regulations of the U.S. Environmental Protection Agency (2005) and the U.S. Department of Homeland Security (2005) along with state departments of environmental quality (or their equivalent). Analogous to the advice pertaining to the hiring of a radiation safety officer, the highly technical nature of the handling and disposal of toxic chemicals should inspire academic administrators to advocate for the highest credentialing (i.e., master's or doctoral-level education and training in chemistry or related areas) and competence in a college or university environmental safety officer.

I am unaware of a need for a toxic-substances oversight committee under most institutional policies; however, it is best for an environmental safety officer to establish good relationships with faculty and staff in the areas of toxic-chemical use and disposal relative to teaching and research. Such interactions can be codified through policies for the use and disposal of toxic chemicals. During development, policy drafts should be reviewed by research committees commonly established through faculty governance bodies.

DANGEROUS DRUGS

Various potent drugs are useful tools in biological teaching and research. When required drugs have a high abuse potential they may be categorized as "Scheduled Drugs" by the U.S. Drug Enforcement Administration (2005) of the Department of Justice under the Controlled Substances Act of 1970. The procurement, use, and disposal of such drugs should be regulated through institutional policies that come under the purview of a pharmacist, physician, veterinarian, or equivalent individual. Akin to oversight of toxic-chemical use, relevant safety officers should establish rapport with faculty governance committees relative to the development of policies for the legitimate use of dangerous drugs in teaching and research.

At this point, we move from research modalities, techniques, and substances to a final set of topics including research misconduct and sexual harassment.

Research and Scholarly Misconduct

Under recently revised regulations (*Code of Federal Regulations,* Department of Health and Human Services, 2005b), academic institutions have had to update policies on the handling of misconduct in research and scholarship. And, while compliance is only necessary for federally sponsored research, most institutions will choose to apply policies to all research and scholarship regardless of whether it is funded extramurally or not.

The U.S. Office of Research Integrity (2006) is the federal government's contact for research misconduct, which is defined as the fabrication, falsification, or plagiarism of information during the proposing, conducting, or reporting of research and its results. In some institutions, research misconduct may extend to the violation of policies related to other compliance areas (e.g., research involving human subjects and animals), and some chief research officers find such extensions useful in prosecuting violators.

The Office of Research Integrity has produced and posted on its website, two documents that are essential to the development of policies and procedures for handling scientific misconduct: *Model Policy for Responding to Allegations of Scientific Misconduct* (1997) and *Model Procedures for Responding to Allegations of Scientific Misconduct* (1997). The documents cover areas such as rights and responsibilities of the institution, whistleblowers (i.e., persons making allegations of misconduct), and respondents (i.e., persons accused of misconduct), along with detailed instructions on the conduct of inquiries (i.e., determining if there is sufficient evidence for a formal investigation) and investigations (i.e., determining guilt through a preponderance of evidence). The documents also define the roles of the institution's research integrity officer (typically the chief research officer) and deciding official (typically the chief academic officer) in research misconduct inquiries and investigations.

The prosecution of research misconduct is serious business and in my experience is accompanied by gut-wrenching sessions with respondents and others associated with any given case. But establishing policies and procedures for research misconduct—along with the resolve to follow through with allegations—has a moral force that is only matched by cases of sexual harassment, policies for which will be considered next.

Sexual Harassment

Sexual harassment is sexual discrimination, which is a violation of Title VII of the Civil Rights Act of 1964. The act's tenets are enforced through the U.S. Office of Equal Employment Opportunity Commission (EEOC, 2006). According to the EEOC, sexual harassment involves, "unwelcome sexual advances, requests for sexual favors, and other verbal or physical conduct of a sexual nature . . . when submission to or rejection of this conduct explicitly or implicitly affects an individual's employment, unreasonably interferes with an individual's work performance or creates an intimidating, hostile or offensive work environment." Language on the EEOC website (2005) also indicates that 1) the victim may be of any gender, 2) the victim may be a direct report or supervisor or any other agent of the firm, institution, or organization, or indeed, a nonemployee permitted into the workplace, 3) harassment does not have to cause economic or bodily harm, and 4) the conduct of the harasser must be unwelcome.

Also, according to the EEOC (2006), sexual harassment may be categorized as occurring under quid pro quo (i.e., where exchange of favors is implied either implicitly or explicitly) arrangements or as a result of a hostile or abusive environment. The latter is typically judged seriously if it is pervasive and severe and may include sexual innuendos, sexually suggestive or offensive signs, graffiti or pictures, discriminatory intimidation, insults, or ridicule.

Policies for dealing with sexual harassment should explicitly address the following areas:

- The link of sexual harassment to discrimination, particularly as defined in federal and state discrimination statutes
- Definition of quid pro quo
- A definition and examples of a hostile environment
- The responsibilities of all institutional personnel to report sexual harassment
- The office responsible for receiving and prosecuting cases of sexual harassment (e.g., office of affirmative action)
- Limits of confidentiality of inquiries and investigations related to charges of sexual harassment
- Consensual relationships, particularly those occurring among faculty members and students

Once policies are in place, the institution should establish mechanisms (e.g., workshops, seminars, orientation sessions) for introducing and reinforcing sexual harassment policies. Faculty members, in particular, need reminders of their obligations in this most important area of institutional life.

A wise research university dean was known to regularly remind faculty members and department chairs that the university "is not a dating service." Having effective sexual harassment policies, procedures, and reminder sessions goes a long way in reinforcing an institution's pledge to protect its community from this particularly insidious form of discrimination.

Besides the chapter to follow—on conflict of interest and commitment—you may now be wondering about other policies that might be deemed ethics-based, such as those involved in antidiscrimination in hiring and promotion and affirmative action (social justice), occupational health and safety (physical well-being), and extramural contracting (fiduciary integrity). Actually, the list goes on and on, but I have chosen those policy domains that impact predominantly faculty members and students. Fortunately, for the academic administrator, questions and concerns related to essentially employment-focused policies benefit from opportunities to partner with units, which are typically contained within business and administration units of higher-education institutions (e.g., offices of affirmative action, facilities management, human resources). In my experience, professionals in such units are eagerly willing to assist administrators on the academic side of the house.

Having considered a range of ethics-based policy issues of direct interest to academic administrators, it is now time to move on to what is a related and perhaps more nettlesome area: conflicts of interest and commitment. So, without further ado, let's move on.

Conflicts of Interest
and Commitment

"No conflict—no interest!" was the reply given by a research administrator when asked to describe his institution's policy on conflict of
interest. Although this response may seem glib, it reflects one understanding of the problem and serves as a good starting point for understanding the issues involved in managing conflicts of interest.
—DAVID A. BLAKE (1941–), American pharmacologist
and medical and pharmaceutical educator

Conflict of interest and commitment—the words may conjure up
thoughts of unethical and illegal behaviors. But conflicts of interest and commitment are inherent in many activities related to the
teaching, research, and service missions of colleges and universities. Indeed,
research administrators have been known to suggest that without conflict
(Blake, 1993), interest and commitment diminish. And, as we will note
below, conflicts of interests do not necessarily have to be eliminated. But,
they must be managed through careful and objective sets of evaluations to
ensure the best interests of the institution and its faculty, students, and
staff.

To begin, we'll consider conflicts of interest and commitment conceptually, offering some broad-based examples of each. This will be followed

by discussions of the occurrence of conflicts of interest and commitment among the areas of teaching, research, and service.

The discussions will relate primarily to faculty members, but there will also be key references to students and staff—both exempt and non-exempt.* But first, let's make sure we are all on the same page about the concepts of conflicts of interest and commitment.

Conflicts of Interest

Conflict of interest—putting one's private interests ahead of an institution, to the detriment of the latter, assumes assorted guises for different players in an academic setting. For faculty members, conflicts of interest may occur in any one of their roles as teachers, researchers or scholars, and service providers. Students, unless they are also serving as employees of the university, are generally immune from institutional policies related to conflicts of interest and commitment. However, students who assume leadership positions in institutionally sanctioned organizations or student governance bodies take on special mantles of responsibility relative to their appointed duties. For staff, conflicts of interest may affect daily responsibilities.

The University of Arkansas Campus Council (1992)—representing a coalition of faculty, student, and staff organizations—developed examples of *potential* conflicts of interest and several are paraphrased below for illustrative purposes:

1. Employees or immediate family members own, manage, or are otherwise connected businesswise with private or public organizations that have dealings with the institution.
2. Instructors of record require purchase of materials by students when the former derive direct or indirect financial benefits.
3. Faculty or staff members receive fees for professional services including consulting, honoraria, royalties, or expert testimony.

---

*In many institutions, the designation "exempt employees" pertains to individuals whose work can be categorized as at least eighty percent executive, administrative, or professional. Under the Fair Labor Standards Act (2006), institutions are not required to pay exempt employees overtime for working more than forty hours in a workweek. In contrast, non-exempt employees are covered by the Fair Labor Standards Act (2006), which requires institutions to provide overtime compensation for time worked more than forty hours in any workweek. In some higher education institutions and states, exempt equates to non-classified employees and non-exempt equates to classified employees, although there may be specific exceptions in the rules governing selected classified staff.

4. Employees accept personal payments, income, gifts, or other benefits from organizations that propose or sponsor research at the institution.
5. Faculty or staff members solicit or receive personal remuneration from extramural agencies for institutionally conducted research.
6. Employees benefit from technology patented or licensed through the institution.
7. Researchers have financial interests in entities that sponsor institutional research.
8. Employees or immediate family members have direct commercial or financial interests in employee's research or transfer of technology resulting from that research.
9. Employees or immediate family members have financial interests in institutional decisions made by or influenced by employees.
10. Faculty or staff use university facilities for personal or commercial activities.
11. Employees are involved in the appointment, promotion, supervision, or management of immediate family members.
12. Faculty or staff members accept gifts or gratuities or payments for advertising endorsements because of their institutional positions.
13. Employees are influenced by interests outside of the institution relative to their publication and dissemination of research or scholarly results.

If you were to share such a list with a group of faculty members, several might remark, "Wait a minute! We know of many exceptions to the cases cited above—exceptions that were sanctioned through supervisors who were guided by institutional policies and procedures." And, indeed they would be right, which I attempted to signal by emphasizing the word "potential" in the preface paragraph. Thus, we would be reminded of a principle codified in government statutes and typical institutional policies: conflicts of interest do not necessarily have to be eliminated; many conflicts of interest—recognizing the best interests of an institution, faculty, students and staff—can be managed through the use of careful and objective sets of evaluations, which we will consider in later sections of this chapter. But, first let's consider common understandings on the issue of conflicts of commitment.

Conflicts of Commitment

Conflict of commitment—diverting one's time or interest from activities understood by supervisor and employee as core responsibilities—is relevant to faculty members and staff, but only for students who are simultaneously employed by the institution. Certain conflicts of commitment may also pose or be defined as conflicts of interest, but below are some examples of *potential* conflicts of commitment, again, paraphrasing examples offered by the University of Arkansas Campus Council (1992):

1. Employees are engaged in outside business activities.
2. Faculty members and staff devote time and efforts to extramural entities, including nonprofit agencies that interfere with obligations, duties, and responsibilities at the institution.
3. Employees provide expert testimony in cases that may harm the university.
4. Faculty or staff members provide gratis scientific and technical expertise to commercial entities.
5. Employees engage in the teaching of credit or noncredit courses, seminars, or workshops for other educational institutions or businesses.

Given the above examples and considering the mythical group of faculty alluded to above, they might remark about exceptions to the above examples, and we would be reminded that analogous to conflicts of interest, apparent conflicts of commitment can sometimes be managed through careful and objective sets of evaluations. In cases of the management of conflicts of commitment, however, the primary source of guidance is institutional policies. Overall, therefore, it will be important to delve more specifically into conflicts of interest and commitment relative to an institution's teaching, research, and service missions. But first, we need to consider more explicitly the applicability of relevant institutional policies and procedures to different categories of employees.

Conflicts of Interest and Commitment
Relative to Institutional Roles

The examples and cases used in the following sections apply primarily to faculty members but can also apply to exempt staff. How they apply relative to non-exempt personnel merits further attention.

Differences between non-exempt and exempt personnel are sometimes lost on academicians. For the record, full-time non-exempt personnel are generally employed on standard forty-hour-per-week schedules that are guided by state and federal statutes relative to overtime obligations and overtime-pay regulations. Generally speaking, full-time non-exempt employees do not conduct institutional work beyond their forty-hour per week assignments. It is logical, therefore, that non-exempt persons' time and commitments beyond their forty-hour work weeks be their own. Thus, non-exempt institutional employees who hold other jobs on their own time will generally be permitted to do so without prior approval, although institutional policies may require that such commitments be disclosed and do not impact the employees' presence, performance, or punctuality in their institutional jobs.

Conditions for employment change dramatically when going from non–exempt to exempt positions, including appointments held by faculty members and faculty serving in administrative posts. And, for purposes of emphasis, I have adopted the "faculty member model" for additional discussion.

Numerous faculty workload studies—completed with self-reported data—have been conducted since the 1950s and indicate that full-time university faculty (i.e., primarily in tenure and tenure-track positions) work more than fifty hours per week. In a recent national study (Zimbler, 2001), the average workweek for full-time instructional faculty and staff was reported as fifty-three hours. When the workweek was broken down into the time spent on teaching, research, and service, the majority of effort was in the area of teaching (57 percent) with the remaining time devoted to research, administration, and other activities. Thus, faculty members typically have robust workloads, and in my experience, those who are truly integrated scholars (see chapter 7) spend sixty or more hours per week in their professional responsibilities. Accordingly, it behooves supervisors—chairs or heads, deans, and central administrators— to think carefully about approvals of responsibilities beyond full-time academic employment.

Recognizing that most faculty members are employed on nine-month contracts, there is commensurate flexibility relative to employment during the summer months. However, if faculty members or exempt staff seek overload assignments within an institution for compensation during the academic year, they will typically require approvals through their supervisors. If outside work is contemplated during the academic year, prior approval by supervisors (i.e., department chair or head and / or dean) is a common requirement for faculty members and exempt staff in higher-education institutions.

Responsible supervisors know that extramural responsibilities may provide benefits to students and the state, through modern and relevant concepts and examples being introduced into the classroom, laboratory, or studio; good will toward the institution; and results of research that advance economic development. However, the management of apparent conflicts of interest and commitment require thoughtful discussion and decision making based on careful assessments of potential harm and benefit, which I will describe in the following sections, focusing on the teaching, research, and service efforts of faculty members and, where relevant, exempt staff.

Interests and Commitments in Teaching

Faculty members and other instructors of record (e.g., teaching assistants), with the concurrence of departmental and institutional curricula committees or bodies, are largely responsible for the content and learning strategies incorporated into courses. These are awesome responsibilities that have potential for conflicts of interest. Most commonly, occasions arise when faculty wish to use materials they have developed that may provide personal remuneration.

The required use in courses of textbooks or other works written by instructors has been a sensitive topic in many institutions. Accordingly, many institutions have adopted policies such as those in effect at the University of Arkansas (UA Faculty Handbook, 2004), which stipulate the following (nearly verbatim):

- Faculty members must disclose the conflict of interest in writing and obtain prior written approval from department chair and dean to require the purchase of their own proprietary materials by their students or to require the purchase of any other materials for which the faculty member receives compensation (including, but not limited to, publishers' incentive payments for textbook adoption).
- The request for approval must include a description of the materials and a justification for their use.
- The request must state the provision made for disposition of revenues and royalties from the sales of the materials. These revenues must be paid to a unit not related to or associated with the

faculty member, but one that will benefit student welfare at the university.

■ Consistent with the deadline for reporting outside employment, faculty members must provide a satisfactory accounting of remuneration and disposition of revenues and royalties acceptable to their dean relative to materials required for institutional student purchase during the preceding year.

Another potential source of conflicts of interest in teaching relate to student assignments by instructors. A conflict of interest exists when faculty assign coursework (e.g., projects, reports) that benefits the nonacademic endeavors of individuals making the assignment, their families, or their friends. For example, requiring students to conduct primary or secondary research benefiting an instructor's or their families' or friends' private business would involve an inherent conflict of interest. This conflict exists even when there are justifiable educational purposes to assignments and indirect, as compared to direct benefit to the instructor or his or her family or friends. Management of such conflicts might be approached through the processes described under the "Interests and Commitments in Research" section below.

Beyond book adoptions and student assignments, major conflicts of interest and commitment may occur when faculty members contemplate teaching assignments beyond their normal responsibilities either at their home institution or at other institutions. In the former case, the conflict of commitment is easily managed by the policy and procedures alluded to earlier.

Teaching extramurally, however, does not have the same fail-safe mechanism. Thus, proposals of this type need scrupulous consideration. For example, assuming a full-time teaching position while holding another full-time position at a given institution would generally be prohibited, and faculty are wise to consult with supervisors before taking on any extramural teaching obligations.

Other less egregious conflicts of commitment and interest may arise relative to extramural teaching engagements, and it is important that faculty members follow institutional policy when such arrangements are proposed. At a time when we have experienced a proliferation of distance-education institutions, the disclosure and management of potential teaching conflicts of interest and commitment have never been more relevant.

As challenging as managing conflicts of interest and commitment in teaching can be, the parallel management issues in research can be even more complicated and are considered next.

Interests and Commitments in Research

Among the three key elements of most college and university missions—teaching, research, and service—research and its pursuit provides the greatest challenges relative to conflicts of interest and commitment. Specifically, the challenges revolve primarily around matters of 1) time and professional commitments, 2) financial and business interests, and 3) intellectual property ownership. Let's consider each separately.

TIME AND PROFESSIONAL COMMITMENTS

Given the earlier discussion about the extensive time commitments of high-quality integrated scholars (i.e., sixty or more hours per week), requests for approval related to consulting and other outside employment deserve careful attention. And, institutional policy should address clearly the limits on outside work and bases for judgments and approvals by supervisors.

While no specific time limits may be noted in institutional policy, approved amounts should be consistent with likely judgments of reasonable peers. If a faculty professional is acknowledged to work up to sixty hours or more per week fulfilling their regular responsibilities, is it reasonable to contemplate working another thirty to forty hours per week extramurally without conflict with institutional employment? One can imagine how reasonable peers would answer such a question. Accordingly, many universities set a reasonable limit of one day (or eight hours) per week for outside employment of faculty and exempt staff members. In my view, this is an upper rule of thumb that supervisors should consider in assessing disclosures that come from faculty or exempt staff. But, when the requests in the one-day-per-week category are requested, I generally recommend that supervisors take the opportunity to discuss the proposed commitments relative to whether there will likely be pressures upon the faculty or exempt staff person to engage beyond the agreed-to limits.

On the conflict-of-commitment side of outside employment, I believe that it is also important for supervisors to explore the relationship of institutional professionals with outside agencies. It is common for faculty and other professionals to enter into consulting arrangements. However, sometimes outside employment is proposed that involves line or staff responsibility in a commercial firm or other institution. For example, it is not uncommon for faculty to be offered positions as board member, president, vice-president, or director of research in start-up firms. In such instances, it behooves supervisors to judge whether the proposed involvements have the potential for abuse in time or commitment. In some instances, such as a start-up company sponsored through a federal Small Business Innovation Research grant (2005), the faculty grantee or principal investigator (PI) may only serve as chief executive officer of the grant-related firm if he or she is employed less than fifty percent in their academic post. In contrast, faculty PIs involved with federal Small Business Technology Transfer Research grants (2005) may assume an executive position and still retain full-time employment with their university (i.e., assuming such a relationship is approved by the academic employer).

Even if roles are not specifically prohibited, supervisors should be very thoughtful in their assessments of the abilities of faculty or exempt staff to adequately handle the dual responsibilities of full-time institutional employment and employment as a line officer in a commercial or other firm. Of course, one ameliorating mechanism for addressing such potential conflicts is for institutional employees to assume reduced appointments at the institution. The level of reduction becomes a matter of administrative judgment based on the best interests of the institution.

Approved outside employment may include financial and business interests that present conflicts of interest. We'll consider this matter next.

FINANCIAL AND BUSINESS INTERESTS

When faculty or exempt staff members conduct institutionally based research that includes potential benefits to firms in which they or their immediate family members have significant financial or other business interests, disclosures and supervisor assessments are required relative to potential conflicts of interest. In the case of sponsored research, the disclosures and evaluations are a part of the proposal preapproval process conducted through an institution's sponsored project office or equivalent. The requirements for disclosure and review emanate from federal regulations developed in 1995, but the disclosure and review processes may have been adopted for all research as should be codified in institutional policy.

Briefly, the disclosure and review process revolves around understandings of "significant financial interest" (i.e., generally deemed to be more than 5 percent) and the potential for conflicts of interest. In cases of significant conflicts of interest, appropriate management may call for a memorandum of understanding (MOU) between affected parties (e.g., an investigator and graduate students who may be assigned to projects that may benefit a commercial firm owned wholly or in part by the investigator). The MOUs may be developed with the help of the institution's conflict-of-interest committee and require supervisory approval. Violations of MOUs may trigger procedures codified through the institution's research and scholarly misconduct policies and procedures, as noted in chapter 21.

Investigator financial and business interests more often than not involve intellectual property ownership, and this topic is considered next.

INTELLECTUAL PROPERTY OWNERSHIP

Intellectual property represents the fruits of original inquiry and creative efforts, which may include algorithms; books or papers; chemicals and devices; drawings; films; genetically modified animals, microorganisms, and plants; ideas or theories; manuscripts; maps; recordings; software; and works of art. Ownership of intellectual property is governed by federal intellectual property laws and regulations, state law, and institutional policies—in cases of institutional employees.

For most copyrighted intellectual property (i.e., in force regardless of federal registration and in effect for the creator's life plus seventy years) arising out of teaching, research, and other scholarly or creative activities (e.g., books, recordings, and works of art), institutions will not typically exercise any right of ownership, whether or not the copyrighted work is federally registered. Judgments about ownership may change when significant institutional resources were required to produce the intellectual property (e.g., on-line course materials) or when computer software is created, and then ownership, licensure, and the splitting of royalties would be determined on a case-by-case basis or where otherwise determined by contract or institutional policy (i.e., work for hire).

Intellectual property that can be patented (i.e., novel, useful, and reduced to practice and protected for twenty years from the date of application) or otherwise protected legally (e.g., processes and products typically derived from scientific research) will usually be subject to claims of institutional ownership as defined through institutional policy. However, most institutions will permit investigators to become financial beneficiaries of such intellectual property if the institution enters into license agreements with a commercial firm and royalties or other fees result. Conflicts of interest arise when institutional faculty or exempt staff members do not abide by relevant institutional patent and copyright policies.

Sometimes, investigators state that they would rather not bother with patenting issues relative to intellectual property that may have resulted from grants sponsored by the federal government. In truth, investigators have no choice. Under the Bayh-Dole Act of 1980, institutions receiving federal funds are obliged to protect and attempt licensing and commercialization of intellectual property emanating from federal government-sponsored research. Thus, it behooves all relevant investigators and their supervisors to abide by these directives, which should be codified in institutional policy.

Some of the considerations noted above apply to institutional faculty and exempt staff members' service efforts, which we will consider next.

Interests and Commitments in Service

Faculty and exempt staff members who perform service outside an institution need to be cognizant of conflicts of interest and commitments primarily in the areas of use of the institution's identity and time, respectively. We'll consider each of these situations separately.

IDENTITY AND COMMITMENTS

It is commendable that faculty and exempt staff members contribute services to community and professional organizations or in certain instances—commercial firms. Occasionally, however, entities being served may take liberties with the services provided and expropriate the institution's identity or reputation to advance their own causes or profits. In cases I have been close to, commercial institutions adopted institutional messages and logos to insinuate an endorsement of their commercial services or products without expressed permission. Careful assessments of the contextual situations indicated that institution-related professionals were involved innocently. Nevertheless, such situations required considerable effort and time to rectify and offer the following lesson: all institutional personnel should be wary of agencies that might take advantage of the institution during efforts to contribute benevolently to society. Also, personnel need to be cognizant of institutional policies regarding the contracting of the institution with extramural entities. Relevant policies also typically place significant restrictions on the institution contracting with institutional employees or firms in which one or more institutional employees has a 10 percent or greater ownership interest.

Assuming appropriate associations among civic and professional organizations and institutional faculty and exempt staff members, there are also concerns relative to time commitments that we will consider next.

TIME COMMITMENTS

Faculty and exempt staff members are not usually remunerated for services provided to civic and professional organizations. If such payments were contemplated either from nonprofit or for-profit organizations the disclosure and approval considerations noted under the section on research (above) would apply. Assuming no remuneration, outside service can present a conflict of commitment time-wise, and disclosure and approval are required as delineated in earlier sections.

Summarizing, managing, or eliminating conflicts of interest and commitment in teaching-, research-, and service-related efforts calls for a blend of sensitivity to civil norms, an understanding of governmental regulations, and adherence to institutional policies and procedures. It's not rocket science but it does require a dedication to disclosure by faculty and exempt staff members and thoughtful and careful assessments through the institutional chain of command. Neglect or obfuscation of issues related to conflicts of interest and commitment can cause serious liabilities for individuals and the institution.

During my many years of administrative service to research universities, conversations with faculty and staff regarding potential conflicts of interest and commitment have generally started with statements by faculty or staff members such as "The opportunity at hand may provide some personal benefits, but I want to make sure that anything I do is in the best interest of the university and will not jeopardize my position at this institution." Such remarks typically segued into open and honest dialogues, which led to solutions that served the best interests of the institution and the individuals involved.

The best interests of colleges and universities are most effectively served by carefully crafted policies and procedures for implementation that balance individual rights and professional development with institutional advancement. Such advancement is also at the heart of multi-institutional academic consortia that we will consider next.

CHAPTER 23

Multi-institutional Academic Consortia and Related Arrangements

The day has long since passed when a college or university can consider itself a fort of knowledge in a hostile frontierland of ignorance, jealously guarding unto itself its hoard of facts and ideas. Academic isolation has long been impractical; in today's world, it is impossible.
—HERMAN B. WELLS (1902–2000), business educator
and academic administrator (president, Indiana
University, 1938–1962; chancellor, 1962–2000)

In the fifties, the presidents of the Big Ten universities and the University of Chicago, led by Herman Wells, formed the Committee on Institutional Cooperation (CIC), which would become a model for interinstitutional cooperation (1967). As Wells would note in his essay in 1967, "At a time when yesterday's bright new fact becomes today's doubt and tomorrow's myth, no single institution has the resources in faculty or facilities to go it alone. A university must do more than just stand guard over the nation's heritage, it must illuminate the present and help shape the future. This demands cooperation—not a diversity of weaknesses, but a union of strengths"—sage words for colleges and universities, then and now.

This chapter offers some thoughts on interinstitutional cooperative ventures with the CIC as backdrop and a sharing of experiences I have had in recent years in helping to form the Southeastern Conference (SEC) Academic Consortium (SECAC). The lessons learned during the SECAC organizational efforts provide some guidance to academic administrators who may be contemplating parallel institutional affiliations or efforts. I'll end with a section on organizational efforts that deans and other academic administrators have used—across colleges and universities nationally—to assist their administrative duties. But, let's start with a brief review of CIC—its history and accomplishments.

The Remarkable CIC

Emanating from twice-yearly informal discussions of the presidents of what was the Big Ten (Michigan State, Northwestern, Ohio State and Purdue universities and the universities of Illinois, Indiana, Iowa, Michigan, Minnesota, and Wisconsin) and the University of Chicago, came the formation—literally on a set of handshakes—of the CIC in 1958. Now based at the University of Illinois Urbana-Champaign and including Pennsylvania State University, the CIC has developed a nearly fifty-year record of collaboration and cooperation among several of the nation's best universities.

The CIC is led by a board of directors consisting of the provosts of the member institutions. Over the years, CIC initiatives and programs have included cooperative library and computer purchases, faculty leadership development and visiting-scholar programs, collaborative study abroad, and enhanced graduate course access, among several others. Testimony from academic and staff leadership affiliated with the CIC (McFadden Allen and Dumas, 2005) attests to the success of these efforts.

Based on the success of the CIC and the encouragement of the chancellors and presidents of the Southeastern Conference (Auburn, Louisiana State, Mississippi State, and Vanderbilt universities and the universities of Alabama, Arkansas, Florida, Georgia, Kentucky, Mississippi, South Carolina, and Tennessee), the SEC provosts began discussions on the formation of an academic consortium in 2003. Results of those discussions and a firsthand look at the benefits of such a cooperative venture follow.

SECAC and Its Early Benefits

The formation of the SECAC came out of discussions of the SEC provosts during a meeting in Atlanta in October of 2003. At that meeting, the SEC provosts heard from Barbara McFadden Allen, executive director of the CIC, who has had long-time affiliation with the CIC office in Urbana, Illinois. As a result of follow-up study and deliberations, the SEC provosts presented an organizational plan and memorandum of understanding to the SEC chancellors and presidents, which launched the SECAC in 2004. In 2005, the SECAC was formally incorporated as a 501(c)(3) non-profit corporation with responsibility for oversight and administration vested in a board of directors consisting of the chief academic officers of the member institutions. In parallel with the CIC, SECAC member institutions need not participate in every initiative of the parent organization; however, early efforts have suggested that there will be broad-based cooperation.

The SECAC board of directors identified four initiatives for pursuit during 2005–10. For each initiative, a lead institution was designated, and the chief academic officer and his or her relevant designee were charged with leading the initiative efforts. The initiatives include (with their lead institution) library acquisitions and cooperation (University of Kentucky), study abroad (University of Arkansas), faculty leadership (University of South Carolina), and minority recruitment and retention (University of Georgia). The first three are well underway in 2006 and have helped relevant professionals get together and devise methods for collaboration and cooperation. In the study-abroad initiative, for example, a list serve has been established through the University of Tennessee, and SECAC study-abroad initiative officers have become actively engaged in meeting mutually shared challenges.

The faculty leadership initiative has been modeled after a parallel effort conducted for several years by the CIC. Briefly, the initiative recognizes the relative paucity of administratively qualified candidates for posts in our colleges and universities. The plan, therefore, is to identify five or six potential administrative leaders at each member institution and offer them the opportunity to attend, over a one-year period, three or four two-day workshops—on SECAC member campuses—on topics such as academic planning, faculty recruitment and retention, and budgeting. The hope is that faculty members completing the one-year leadership-training program will be much better equipped to compete for academic administrative posts at member institutions and beyond.

Besides the advantages from the specific initiatives, I have derived significant benefits from getting to know my chief academic officer counterparts in the SEC. When questions arise about best practices in administrative areas, it is good to know that you can readily poll a group of friends and colleagues who have a special inclination to respond.

Beyond the direct benefits to the SEC chief academic officers, there is an intention to organize other groups with similar interests (e.g., academic deans) to enhance cooperation and collaboration across the SEC. Similar groups (e.g., chief information officers, graduate deans, international student and scholars services directors) have functioned effectively for several years in the CIC.

With initiatives underway and a plan in place for generating revenue (i.e., annual payments by chief academic officers), the SECAC board of directors has approved a process (i.e., involving a formal request for proposals) for locating and establishing a SECAC office on one of its member campuses. That process should be complete by mid-2006. Where might it all lead? Well, the CIC has an executive director and staff of about fifteen professionals who are well noted for serving what has become a highly valued organization. It is hoped that future SECAC administrators will be able to organize similarly and reap comparable benefits.

Now, I do not wish to imply that organizations such as the CIC and SECAC are the only multi-institutional arrangements of potential benefits to academic administrators. Indeed, there are other groups that serve academic administrators well, and I offer survey comments about some of these groups in the following section.

Other Multi-institutional Academic Administrative Organizations and Arrangements

Chief academic officers, vice-provosts for research (or their equivalent), deans in arts and sciences and a number of professional areas, and chairs or heads in many disciplines have organized themselves for periodic meetings on administrative development and related efforts. Following are short descriptions and contact information on some representative groups:

- The Association of American Universities (AAU, 2006) has sixty U.S. and two Canadian institutional members (membership is by invitation-only). Through AAU, a set of organizational groups (i.e., chief academic officers, graduate deans, and senior research officers) have been developed that meet periodically to support academic administrative interests.
- The National Association of State Universities and Land-Grant Colleges (NASULGC, 2006) represents 215 institutions, which includes 76 land-grant universities. Through NASULGC, a set of councils have been organized (i.e., councils of academic,

extension, continuing-education, public-service, research-policy, and graduate-education officers) that meet twice yearly to serve the academic administrative developmental interests of the membership.

■ Agriculture and human environmental sciences (or equivalent) deans and department chairs and heads receive administrative development support through the Academic Programs Section of the Commission of Food, Environment and Renewable Resources of NASULGC (2006).

■ Deans and department heads of architecture departments may participate in administratively oriented sessions organized yearly through the Association of Collegiate Schools of Architecture (2006).

■ Arts and sciences deans in relevant accredited units in colleges and universities receive assistance in administrative development matters through the Council of Colleges of Arts and Sciences (CCAS, 2006), which conducts seminars for deans and department chairs and provides opportunities for networking, among other services. CCAS has more than 480 institutional members in the United States, Puerto Rico, Guam, France, Mexico, and the United Kingdom.

■ In education, deans rely on two organizations for networking and developmental assistance in administrative matters (see bibliography for website information): the American Association of Colleges of Teacher Education (2006) and the Council of Academic Deans from Research Education Institutions (2006).

■ Deans of engineering have organized the Engineering Dean's Council (EDC, 2006) through the American Association of Engineering Education. The EDC meets three times yearly, and presentations and discussions are offered on engineering education issues, including academic administrative matters. Chairs or heads of engineering departments are assisted in their administrative work through the following associations (see bibliography for website information): American Institute of Chemical Engineers (2006), American Society of Civil Engineers (2006), American Society of Mechanical Engineers (2006), Institute of Biological Engineering (2006), Institute of Electrical and Electronics Engineers (for electrical and computer engineering) (2006), Institute of Industrial Engineers (2006), and the Minerals, Metals and Materials Society (TMS for short,2006).

■ In law, the Association of American Law Schools (2006), supports networking and other administrative development information and services to deans and law faculty members.

In summary, we've considered a range of institutional collaborations and arrangements that can assist academic administrators in carrying out their roles and responsibilities. We now move on to a chapter on partnerships with academic, corporate, government, and non-government organizations that benefit individual faculty, students, and staff as well as institutional missions.

CHAPTER 24

Partnerships with Academic, Corporate, Government, and Non-government Organizations

> Business—and this means not just the business of commerce but the business of education, the business of government, the business of medicine—is a team activity. And, always, it takes a team to win.
> —ANDREW S. GROVE (1936–), electrical engineer (PhD, University of California Berkeley), founder and one-time president, chief executive officer, and chairman of the board of Intel Corporation

B e you a department chair, director, dean, or provost, at some time or another you will be involved in institutional partnerships—their conceptualization, development, or elimination. It matters little what field or discipline you represent—from the sciences to engineering to the social sciences, arts, or humanities—the development and formation of partnerships are common occurrences in twenty-first-century colleges and universities.

This chapter was crafted to characterize partnerships between academic institutions per se as well as partnerships of higher-education institutions with corporate, government, and nongovernmental organizations. We'll consider the advantages and pitfalls of such relationships, along with some examples of successes, follies, and failures—suitably disguised to prevent embarrassment. So, let's get started with interinstitutional partnerships.

Partnerships among Academic Institutions

In the chapters 8, 16, and 23 collectively, we considered multi-institutional academic consortia and some of their advantages, along with academic administrative developmental benefits derived through programs sponsored by professional associations and other organizations. While existing multi-institutional academic consortia (e.g., Committee on Institutional Cooperation representing the Big Ten universities and the University of Chicago) and institutional associations (e.g., Association of American Universities) offer established frameworks, one should consider interinstitutional partnerships that typically begin in the mind of a faculty person or develop out of the discussions of several faculty members who then come to academic administrators with ideas for partnerships.

Typically, the bases for higher-education interinstitutional agreements stem from major research collaborations among several investigators. Examples of such collaborations include centers established and funded through the National Institutes of Health and the National Science Foundation. An example is the highly successful NSF-funded (2000–2010) Center for Semiconductor Physics in Nanostructures (C-SPIN), which involves faculty and students at the University of Arkansas and the University of Oklahoma. The success of C-SPIN has come from an effective sharing of expertise across areas that would unlikely to have been developed entirely at either institution independently. The strength of the partnership also resulted from capitalizing on the complementary strengths of people and programs at both institutions.

As digitization and telecommunication systems continue to advance—making linkages across hundreds of miles more and more feasible—the desirability and practicality of centers such as C-SPIN will continue to expand. And here's an added benefit: major interinstitutional partnerships will allow the development of joint degrees across institutions—with attendant advantages to students.

Interinstitutional partnerships present opportunities to compete for funding at levels impossible for institutions acting alone. But, such partnerships require extra efforts to work out details of how funds will be shared. These efforts must occur well ahead of any funding decision and require the close collaboration of investigators with their sponsored-programs offices as well as cooperation among such offices at the institutions. In my experience, however, the efforts are well worth it, and what may at first seem to be "insurmountable paperwork" is ultimately manageable.

Funding opportunities need not be the only bases for interinstitutional collaborations. Sometimes, successful partnerships emerge from unusual circumstances. Take, for example, partnerships among agricultural colleges in the northern and southern hemispheres—partnerships focused on varietal development of food plants. Imagine a cooperative program that allows two growing seasons rather than one per year. This is the natural advantage of such an arrangement that I witnessed playing out in the 1990s between institutions in the Pacific Northwest and Chile.

I alluded above to a pitfall of partnerships when there is incomplete understanding or misunderstanding of funding arrangements. Funding, however, is not the only potential frailty of interinstitutional partnerships. Several years ago, I witnessed the collapse of a partnership for the joint education of undergraduate students when a unique sociopolitical event caused one institution to precipitously withdraw support from the project—to the detriment of the students of that institution. Fortunately, the remaining partner was able to provide services unilaterally to its students for one semester to minimize harm. In such instances, it is important that involved administrators have the willingness to take quick and decisive actions. In the case in question, the partnership was quickly dissolved by taking advantage of an appropriate dissolution clause in the interinstitutional memorandum of understanding.

So, what components enter into a formula for success of interinstitutional partnerships? Here are some key elements on my list:

- Collaborative, accomplished, and unselfish faculty and staff members
- Clear understanding of the benefits
- Administrative champions
- Understanding and commitments to cost sharing
- Courage to stay the course in times of adversity
- Knowing when a relationship needs severing and having mechanisms to make it happen readily

Actually, many if not all of these elements are important in other partnerships, including university-corporate partnerships, which we will consider next.

University-Corporate Partnerships

Partnerships between academic institutions and corporations can provide unique and enriching opportunities for faculty members, students, and staff. These partnerships also present some of the most vexing challenges among all academic partnerships. We'll consider both sides of the coin.

The opportunities afforded through academic-corporate partnerships are many, but here are a few of the ones that head my list:

- Internships for students
- Post-education employment opportunities for students
- Increased research funding for the academic partner, and sometimes for the collaborating partners as well (e.g., Small Business Innovation Research grants)
- Enhanced opportunities for intellectual-property development
- Possibilities for new company formation and enhanced regional · or state-wide economic development
- The sharing of resources, especially access by corporate partners to college- or university-based equipment

I have personally witnessed these opportunities and the strengths of academic-corporate partnerships—many of which are undoubtedly familiar to the academic administrative readership of this volume. But, as they say, "Your strengths are your weaknesses." Thus, for every opportunity referred to above, I can point to failings I have also witnessed. Here are some specifics—patterned after the above list :

- When internships become surrogates for cheap labor—beware! Academic-corporate partnerships should include carefully crafted descriptions of responsibilities of students and mentors along with quality-assurance elements (e.g., academic oversight and assessments). Students must not be exploited. In one case of which I am aware, students were "employed" in corporate firms in a nearby state with "wages" going back to an academic unit that used the money to create a slush fund. The activities led to criminal charges.
- The potential for post-employment opportunities should not evolve into sets of automatic expectations either by the students or the corporate partners. These failings can occur—to the detriment of students—when representatives of the academic or corporate entities envision some benefit through the "placement" of

students without the them being apprised of the range of opportunities that may be available to them.

■ Academic-corporate partnerships are clearly associated with
increased opportunities for research grants to academic entities
from the corporate partners. However, if the grants come without provisions for indirect costs or are disguised as corporate
gifts, the institution winds up subsidizing the corporate entities,
which is unfortunate for private institutions and unconscionable
for public institutions.

■ Increased opportunities for intellectual-property development,
including new materials, methods, processes, reports, and works
of art, represent great benefits. But, care must be taken to protect
author or investigator rights through copyright and patent protection. If the partnership involves a proposal for production of
works for hire with full rights going to the corporate partner,
then the value of the partnership should be reevaluated.

■ Academic-corporate partnerships may enhance opportunities for
academic institutions to benefit from new business affiliations
(e.g., through licensed intellectual property). Such benefits, however, need to be clearly delineated to prevent conflicts of interest
and commitment as noted in chapter 22.

■ Academic-corporate partnerships, particularly those with smaller
business entities, often come with the advantage to the corporate
entity of having access to sophisticated equipment possessed by
the academic partner. However, if there is not a documented and
well-understood quid pro quo for both entities, critical questions
may be raised, particularly in cases of public institutions (i.e., by
legislative or judicial bodies).

Given the challenges noted above, are academic-corporate partnerships worth it? On balance, the answer has to be "Yes"! But, the development of such partnerships takes much foresight and care. Perhaps as much
as partnerships with government and non-government entities that we
will consider next.

Partnerships of Academic Institutions with Government and Non-government Entities

Given the title of this section, particularly the academic institution–
government partnerships, some cynical academics would cry, "Don't do it!"
But, there are distinct advantages that may accrue from such partnerships,

particularly those with federal and state agencies. Following are some possibilities, along with advantages and disadvantages:

- Cooperative agreements among academic institutions and government entities are similar to research grants but provide for more direction by the funding agency during the course of the research. Cooperative agreements have been used by federal agencies such as the U.S. Department of Agriculture (USDA) and the Environmental Protection Agency and can lead to opportunities that otherwise might not be possible. On the academic institution side, successful cooperative agreements require faculty members and staff to transcend the stereotypical model of independent scholarship and develop a level of comfort with the direction of some research coming from an outside agency. One advantage of cooperative agreements is their enhanced likelihood for funding renewals because of direct linkages to objectives espoused by the funding agency.

- Partnerships with state (e.g., health and human services) and federal funding agencies (e.g., U.S. Department of Defense [DOD]) for training services are commonly encountered among higher-education institutions. The drawbacks to these arrangements can include a paucity of curriculum control by the academic institution and its faculty along with unacceptable in-kind cost-sharing (e.g., faculty or staff time) expectations by the government agency. I have also seen partnerships like this sour when training evaluations were not up to government expectations. A further disadvantage for the academic partner accrues when a partnering unit or program becomes overly dependent on funding from the training program.

- Block-grant partnerships such as the National Aeronautics and Space Administration Space-Grant Program, Experimental Program to Stimulate Research (i.e., so-called EPSCoR programs imbedded in several federal agencies, including DOD and NSF) and the water resources program of U.S. Geological Survey (USGS, within the U.S. Department of Interior) have for years helped universities support intramural research with varying success. However, the matching requirements of such programs may present significant challenges for academic institutions. In the case of the USGS program, for example, when the matching funding requirements went from one-to-one to two-to-one with the academic institution having to make the disproportionate contribution, fewer institutions continued participation in the program.

■ Academic–federal government agreements may lead to extraordinary opportunities, especially for research universities. Here, I think of the Lawrence Livermore National Laboratory run by the University of California Berkeley for the U.S. Department of Energy (2006); the Lincoln Laboratory at the Massachusetts Institute of Technology (2006), which has conducted national security-related applied-science and technological research since 1951; and the Applied Physics Laboratory at Johns Hopkins University (2006), which operates through a university-related non-profit corporation and conducts greater than $500 million per year of research sponsored by the federal government. The disadvantages to such monumental undertakings include the extensive and far-reaching responsibilities of the academic partner. But, sometimes risks can be mitigated by tripartite or even more complex relationships among higher-education-institution-government-corporate partnerships such as the one crafted recently among the University of California, Berkeley; Bechtel National.; BWX Technologies; and the Washington Group International in their successful bid to run Los Alamos Laboratories through a contract with the U.S. Department of Energy (Field, 2006).

■ Colleges or universities may also have advantages in attracting of federal operations to their campuses. The most notable examples are at land-grant colleges and universities that host USDA units and scientists, the latter of which will frequently have adjunct appointments in colleges of agriculture (or their equivalent) where they may offer courses and mentor students.

The challenges highlighted for academic institution–government partnerships can have parallels in partnerships with non-government organizations (NGOs). The disadvantage in these partnerships is that financial benefits are typically smaller. However, you will find high-quality academic institution–NGO partnerships represented by the block-grant programs of the American Heart Association (2006), the student exchange programs of the Western Commission for Higher Education (2006), the cooperative library agreements mounted through the Greater Western Library Alliance, and initiatives in nuclear physics, information technologies, and coastal research promoted through the Southeastern Universities Research Association (2006), to name just a few.

In summary, partnerships between academic institutions per se as well as partnerships of higher-education institutions and corporate, government, and non-governmental organizations offer many advantages, which make their pursuit an essential component of the teaching, research, and service missions of academic institutions. Administrators, however, must be aware of the challenges faced in such partnerships and take measures to protect the interests of their institutions and their academic community members. This mixed picture also obtains when considering international outreach, which we will consider in the next chapter.

International Outreach

The United States falls short on virtually all indicators of international knowledge, awareness and competence. In a National Geographic-Roper (2002) poll of geographic knowledge among young adults in nine countries, Americans finished next to last. Fewer than twenty-five percent of the Americans surveyed could name four countries that acknowledge having nuclear weapons.

—A Call to Leadership, Report of the NASULGC
Task Force on International Education, 2004

Nothing will better help us secure America's place in the world than a steady stream of bright, culturally astute, and politically savvy graduates from our nation's colleges and universities. To fulfill this goal, graduates will have to have a clear and coherent cosmopolitan view, as suggested in chapter 4. Such a view develops with internationally based experiences that range from language and literature studies to study-abroad experiences to studying and social encounters with multicultural students in internationally-based research and service-learning projects.

If you buy into the philosophy espoused above, you probably also believe that such cosmopolitan experiences not only enrich students but also faculty and staff. Thus, having a strategy for internationalizing campus communities ought to be on the agenda for all colleges and universities in America. And, academic administrators should have roles to play in shaping the strategies as well as implementing plans.

Of course, there are no institutions where internationalization is absent, given the abilities our faculty members have—and increasingly our students—to reach out in learning and research through the Internet. But, to maximize use of resources and to build on strengths—as indicated in earlier sections on planning (i.e., chapters 17 and 18)—it is important to consider the "where," "what," and "how" of internationalization efforts. Let's consider these foci—one at a time.

The "Where" of Internationalization

Academic administrators at all levels should be able to look across their units and answer the following question: What cultural and geographic features characterize the highest-quality academic work we are pursuing internationally? And, while a department or collegiate unit cannot hope to shape an entire institution's internationalization agenda, the units' efforts may contribute significantly to themes and larger initiatives that an institution may pursue.

At the institutional level, a strategic plan ought to exist relative to international efforts. Just as a college or university cannot be all things to all people—academic program-wise—few if any academic institutions can afford a presence in all corners of the world. Planning might evolve around the following types of questions and elaborations:

- Are there places in the world that naturally arise when thinking about the scholarly interests and accomplishments of the institution's faculty and students? Do those locales and interests have special relevance to the nation's and world's needs? Clearly, institutions whose strengths lie in Central Asian and Middle East studies have a huge potential set of contributions to make relative to the sociopolitical realties facing our world community. Similarly, the future socioeconomic importance of countries such as China, India, and Japan make investments in Far East Asian studies attractive, given appropriate faculty strengths and scholarly emphases.

- Do the "where" analyses suggest certain synergistic possibilities? A university that has already developed strengths in Middle East studies, may have also traditionally had efforts in Southern Europe. Might the combined interests be coupled into a Mediterranean studies emphasis?

- Might the presence of certain ethnic influences in an institution's locale or among its alumni suggest efforts in certain areas? I know of one institution that used this rationale and corresponding faculty scholarly contributions to craft an Irish studies program. Such commitments may have special appeal in fund-raising efforts as noted in chapter 18.

Having defined the "where" of internationalization efforts, it is then important to define "what" might be done in special ways to support an institution's mission.

The "What" of Internationalization

Internationalization may contribute to an institution's teaching, research, or service mission or enhance all three components. The trick is to define the "what" that is most important, that builds on current strengths, and that may make the most sense relative to the international partnerships that may be necessary to accomplish institutional goals.

Building on the geographical emphases of initiatives—as I noted above —it is important for institutional leadership to think about what programmatic efforts are best emphasized in given locales. A significant number of universities, for example, have opened or contemplated opening branch campuses in other nations. Many notable efforts have been in China and India. But, making such a decision involves significant investment and potential risk. The investment can be bolstered and risks modulated by partnerships with academically strong and well-established institutions. Accomplished faculty members and insightful foreign-admission officers should be helpful in identifying institutional partnering candidates. Other thoughts on partnering strategies are offered in the last section of this chapter.

If the "what" includes economic-development projects, for example, institutional leaders should consider linkages to government agencies that approve business-related activities. And, development projects in general are facilitated and best supported if additional partnerships are sought with government agencies (e.g., U.S. Agency for International Development in the Department of State) or NGOs (e.g., Heifer International).

With the "where" and "what" in place, let's consider organizational constructs and programs—the "how"—that may assist an institution's internationalization efforts.

The "How" of Internationalization

How does an institution build on its international presence and, indeed, develop a robust internationalization effort? At a recent conference organized by study-abroad officials of institutions in the Southeastern Conference (2005), I heard over and over again, "The commitment to internationalization must come from the very top of the institution and its importance must be espoused often by chief executive and academic officers." Assuming that these officers are informed by recent works on the subject (e.g., *A Call to Leadership,* 2004), a strategic planning effort—perhaps emanating from a college- or university-wide task force—will go a long way in soliciting input across the academic community and in raising consciousness. Reports resulting from such strategic-planning efforts should not only help in planning but also help in identifying programs and resources in implementing recommendations for enhanced internationalization.

Some institutions have established offices or centers in international outreach, with staff and faculty leaders involved in development, education, and research. The best of these units will have designated protocol officers, who are savvy regarding international culture and politics. These officers will assist high-level contacts among the parent institution's leadership and leaders of foreign higher-education institutions and government offices. A protocol officer should also be able to help with visits of foreign dignitaries, providing advice on everything from greeting customs to understanding cultural backgrounds to cuisine to gift giving.

The international office or center should also be a focal point for development activities, including everything from managing visiting-scholar and study-abroad programs to faculty seed-grant programs to coordination of multi-unit initiatives to advice on grant proposal writing and submissions. Such a unit should preferably be led by a faculty person well versed in international scholarship and at a point in her or his career where the desire to reach out and help others along the internationalization road is of paramount importance.

If your institution already has an international office or center of the type noted above—you're lucky. If not, thought should be given to crafting a suitable organizational construct to assist faculty and students in their international pursuits. Paramount in these efforts are study-abroad programs, which have become increasingly important to students in recent years. And, don't forget assistance to students and faculty with the range of postgraduate fellowship programs (e.g., Rhodes and Marshal scholarships, Fulbright and Guggenheim fellowships) that immensely enrich international study and research.

Besides services to U.S. students that are currently enrolled, international offices or centers may offer services to matriculated and incoming international students, including, but not limited to, help with English-as-a-second-language skills, visa applications, and relocation advice and assistance. International service units should work in close harmony with admissions officers both at the undergraduate and graduate levels.

Beyond international offices and centers, institutions need continuing-education centers or colleges (or their equivalent) to assist in areas such as distance-education instructional development, technology and scheduling expertise, media development, and off-campus registration activities that are vital to internationalization efforts. Continuing-education units may house or manage international offices or centers. I have also witnessed international offices or centers in graduate schools and university research divisions.

So, step back, think of the "where," "what," and "how" of internationalization at your college and university and think how you might contribute. If you need further background information consider the NASULGC Report (*A Call to Leadership,* 2004) mentioned earlier or perhaps the works of Biddle (2002) or Wit (2002). I also recommend recent works on study abroad (*Securing America's Future: Global Education for a Global Age,* 2003) and scholarship competitions (McCray, 2005).

Philip G. Altbach (2002), J. Donald Monan, S. J. Professor of Higher Education and director of the Center for International Higher Education at Boston College, sums up internationalization in higher education as follows: "Internationalization is a major trend in higher education. It is also a worldwide phenomenon. And it is widely misunderstood." I hope this chapter and other portions of this book may provide information and insights that may enhance all of our contributions to academic internationalization.

We now make the transition from what many may think of as the "sublime to the ridiculous"—from internationalization to inclement weather. Actually, I was originally going to omit the "weather chapter" until my editor suggested that it might turn out to be "one of the most useful chapters of your entire book." So, here we go with the weather!

CHAPTER 26

Inclement Weather

Everybody talks about the weather, but nobody does anything about it.
—widely attributed to Mark Twain (1835–1910) but probably
derived from a similar assertion by Twain's friend Charles Dudley
Warner (1829–1900), American essayist and novelist, that appeared
in an August 27, 1897, editorial in the Hartford Courant

In chapter 12, we considered the superb contributions that Louisiana State University made to the citizens of Louisiana following Hurricane Katrina. We can only hope that the catastrophic events along the Gulf Coast during August of 2005—especially the hurricane's devastating impact on higher-education institutions in Louisiana and Mississippi—will be a once-in-a-lifetime experience. But, dealing with more routinely encountered inclement-weather events—particularly snow and ice—is the job of many academic administrators especially those who are charged with decisions on closing or modifying schedules of colleges and universities. This chapter was developed primarily for these officers.

There are probably many ways of organizing the topic of administrative responses to inclement weather. But, it seemed useful to consider several major segments: policies, procedures, and implications for the teaching, research, and service missions of colleges and universities. So, let's consider these subtopics, individually.

Inclement-Weather Policies

Definitions of what constitutes inclement weather and attitudes about it vary from one portion of the country to another. I have worked at Northeastern, Upper Midwest, and Pacific Northwest universities where it was a rare event to close or even consider closing a higher-education institution due to ice or snow, in part because of effective snow and ice removal equipment and the procedures of local and state agencies. In other portions of the country (e.g., the Southeast and Southwest), however, ice and snow events are more episodic and therefore more challenging for faculty, staff, and students. Thus, statements about the likelihood of the institution closing due to inclement weather should be incorporated into relevant policies—along with descriptions of options that may be invoked relative to schedule modifications and campus-unit closings.

Policy documents should also deal with the authority of local supervisors to make decisions about unit schedules and closings relative to daytime versus overnight events. Specifically, it makes sense to accord unit supervisors more authority for independent action during daytime events, based on developing information and anxieties expressed by faculty, staff, and students. Inclement-weather policies should also incorporate specific provisions of how and when classes will be cancelled and rescheduled.

At one university where I have worked, it was mandated that faculty members incorporate inclement-weather statements in syllabi of courses relative to class cancellations. In many cases, faculty members simply indicated that if local K-12 schools announced closings (i.e., a more frequent occurrence than that of the relevant university), classes were automatically cancelled and subject to rescheduling at a later time. The syllabus strategy forestalled a great number of problems for academic administrators, who could concentrate their efforts on inclement-weather-policy-related questions and the concerns of faculty members and staff.

As suggested above, inclement-weather policies should contain summaries of procedures used to make decisions about schedule modifications and campus-unit closings. Let's consider this subtopic next.

Responding to Inclement-Weather Events

Standard procedures should be established for responding to inclement-weather events for both overnight and daytime events. The overnight events especially call for central administrative decisions; thus, procedures need to be in place for beginning a new day that may be challenged by inclement weather. Following is a model set of procedures for handling the "overnight weather challenge":

- University staff—particular university-police—are out and about between 3:00 and 5:00 a.m., testing road conditions and determining the potential hazardous nature of travel in the area.
- When the weather threatens the driving safety in the community, a conference call is scheduled for 5:00 a.m. involving the chief academic officer, the chief of police and one of his or her patrol officers, the director of transit and parking, a member of the institution's public-relations staff, and the student-government president or vice-president. The call begins with a report on road conditions as gathered by the police department (or equivalent) and transit officials. Up-to-date weather reports from the National Weather Service (2006) are also part of the conversation.
- Given the best information possible, a decision is made about the institution's status for the day. If road conditions are deemed safe, no action is taken, and the prevailing assumption (according to policy) is that the institution is open as usual.
- If road conditions are marginal but it appears that improvements will occur in the early morning hours, the institution's inclement-

weather policy may be invoked. The policy allows for staff to take up to two hours, as needed to safely arrive at work. No leave time is deducted for staff members who exercise this option, but it is recommended that staff contact their supervisors about their status and expected time of arrival at work.

■ Information about the activation of the inclement-weather policy is posted on the institution's web page, and an announcement is sent to the voice mailbox of all employees who have this service. Weather information is also made available through a recording accessible by telephone and a toll-free number.

■ In cases where the weather has caused hazardous driving conditions, the institution may be closed, and if such hazardous conditions prevail at 5:00 a.m., the closure is for the day.

■ If a closure decision is made, announcements of the institution's closing are given to local radio and TV stations for broadcast. Closing information is also made available through the institution's website, voicemail, and the phone linkage noted earlier.

As indicated above, the inclement-weather policy does not apply to students and faculty relative to class, laboratory, or studio sessions; however, this fact should not signal that the institution is silent on safety concerns for faculty and students in the case of hazardous driving and walking. Rather, institutional policy can require that faculty address inclement-weather contingencies in their syllabi. Syllabi should also contain directions to students on how to contact faculty to determine whether classes are being held and how work may be made up in cases of necessary absence.

The model procedures elaborated above have implications for the academic mission on institutions, but other mission implications should also be considered before completing this chapter and we'll do that next.

The Impact of Inclement Weather on Academic Missions

When I have been in the position of influencing a final decision on institutional closings because of borderline inclement weather that could have had impact on driving conditions, I have had to face the question: "Why don't you just close the university?" As most academic administrators will attest, "We don't 'just close the university' without good reason." Indeed, in one institution where I worked, a single day was worth more than $500,000 in lost productivity. Thus, a closure decision should be made only after due deliberation.

With administrators having appropriate caution about closures, the inclement-weather policy I alluded to earlier—where staff are given a two-hour grace period to come to work—served one institution admirably. Similarly, the flexibility given to faculty members to cancel a class worked well—in my experience. However, always implicit in a decision for class cancellation is a commitment to making up lost work. To act with less diligence threatens the accountability we have to accrediting agencies, students and parents, and—in the case of state institutions—to governmental oversight bodies.

When pressed for advice by students, faculty members, and staff on personal decisions about venturing out under potentially hazardous conditions I always recommend, erring on the safe side. For staff, there is usually accumulated annual leave that can be tapped into. For students, there is the promise of opportunities to make up work—backed by institutional policy (i.e., that should exist) and the authority of deans or higher academic officers to ensure necessary attentiveness to student needs. For faculty members, they can always work at home.

Summarizing, we considered inclement weather from the aspects of policies, procedures, and impacts on academic missions. I hope that I haven't made too big a deal about the topic, but if my editor is right, perhaps I offered some helpful advice. So, while we can't do much about the weather, we can ease its impact when it becomes inclement.

Concluding a volume with a chapter on a somewhat prosaic if not mundane topic cries out for some concluding thoughts. If you are interested, you will find some final musings in the epilogue to follow.

Epilogue

I did not start out to write a book containing twenty-six chapters, but as many authors have noted, a work almost takes on a life of its own during its creation. Thus, while crafting this work, I added some things and deleted much less, and at the end, there was a chapter 26—and a coincidence.

If you are a devotee of Antoine Saint-Exupéry's book, *The Little Prince,* you know that chapter 26 contains an account of the fateful parting of the desert-stranded pilot (based on a personal incident that Antoine de Saint-Exupéry, a legendary flyer, had in 1935 in the Sahara Desert) and the diminutive star traveler. You may also recall what the princely character said to the pilot just before his departure for home (asteroid B-612):

> All men have the stars . . . but they are not the same things for different people. For some, who are travelers, the stars are guides. For others they are no more than little lights in the sky. For others, who are scholars, they are problems. For my businessman they were wealth. . . . You—you alone—will have the stars as no one else has them. . . .
>
> In one of the stars I shall be living. In one of them I shall be laughing. And so it will be as if all the stars were laughing, when you look at the sky at night. . . .
>
> And when your sorrow is comforted . . . you will be content that you have known me. You will always be my friend. You will want to laugh with me. And you will sometimes open your window, so, for that pleasure. . . . And your friends will be properly astonished to see you laughing as you look up at the sky! Then you will say to them, "Yes, the stars always make me laugh!"

I have used this quote many times in referring to alumni and friends of institutions where I have worked—to signal metaphorically how our supporters enjoy greatly the institution's triumphs—laughing with us as it were from their home bases. The reference often brings audience members to tears. In contrast to this concluding allusion and its noted effect on audiences, you may, at end, just be happy that this book is over. But, I hope that it has brought some joy, some inspiration, some good information, and possibly some sage advice that may be useful to you in your work and academic administrative career. I hope, too, that you will take the time to write to me if your experiences might inform future revisions of this work. Certainly, your comments, suggestions, and criticisms are welcome. Bonne chance!

Bibliography

ABET, Inc. Leadership and Quality Assurance in Applied Science, Computing, Engineering, and Technology Education. Baltimore, MD. http://www.abet.org/ (January 20, 2006).

A Call to Leadership: The Role of the President in Internationalizing the University. Report of the NASULGC Task Force on Internationalization. National Association of State Universities and Land-Grant Colleges (NASULGC), 2005. Washington, DC. http://www.nasulgc.org/comm_intprogs.htm (January 10, 2006).

Albert, Adrien. *Selective Toxicity.* 2nd ed. New York: Wiley, 1960.

Altbach, Philip G. "Perspectives on Internationalizing Higher Education." Boston College: Center for International Higher Education, 2002. http://www.bc.edu/bc_org/avp/soe/cihe/newsletter/News27/text004.htm (January 10, 2006).

American Association of Colleges of Teacher Education. Washington, DC. http://www.aacte.org/ (January 3, 2006).

American Heart Association. Washington, DC.http://www.americanheart.org/presenter.jhtml?identifier=1200050 (January 8, 2006).

American Institute of Chemical Engineers. Washington, DC. http://www.aiche.org/ (January 3, 2006).

American Management Association. "E-Learning" Program and Print-version Self-study Courses. New York, NY. http://www.amanet.org/elearn/index.htm and http://www.amanet.org/selfstudy/index.htm (November 6, 2005).

American Society of Civil Engineers. Washington, DC. http://www.asce.org/asce.cfm (3 January 2006).

American Society of Mechanical Engineers. Washington, DC. http://www.asme.org/ (January 3, 2006).

Applied Physics Laboratory. Johns Hopkins University. Laurel, MD. http://www.jhuapl.edu/ (January 8, 2006).

Associated Press Report. "U. Arkansas Deaths Murder-Suicide." August 30, 2000. http://www.cbsnews.com/stories/2000/08/28/national/main228544.shtml (October 30, 2005).

Association of American Law Schools. Washington, DC. http://www.aals.org/ (January 3, 2006).

Association of American Colleges and Universities. Washington, DC. http://www.aacu-edu.org/ (January 20, 2006).

Association of American Universities. Washington, DC. http://www.aau.edu/ (January 2, 2006).

Association of Collegiate Schools of Architecture. Washington, DC. http://www.acsa-arch.org/ (January 3, 2006).

Bacher, Renée, Teresa Devlin, Kristine Calongne, Joshua Duplechain, and Stephanie Pertuit, with a foreword by Sean O'Keefe (chancellor). *LSU in the Eye of the Storm.* Baton Rouge: Louisiana State University, 2005.

Baum, L. Frank. *The Wizard of Oz.* 1900. Reprint, New York: Puffin Books, 1982.

Biddle, Sheila. *Internationalization: Rhetoric or Reality?* New York: American Council of Learned Societies, Occasional Paper No. 56, 2002.

Blake, David A. "Marketing the Results of University Research." *Chronicle of Higher Education* 39 no. 36, (1993): A52.

Botton, Alain de. *The Art of Travel.* New York: Pantheon, 2002.

Boyer, Ernest L. *Scholarship Reconsidered—Priorities of the Professoriate.* Princeton, NJ: The Carnegie Foundation for the Advancement of Teaching, 1990.

Bright, David F., and Mary P. Richards. *The Academic Deanship: Individual Careers and Institutional Roles.* San Francisco: Jossey Bass, 2001.

Buscaglia, Leo. *Living, Loving and Learning.* New York: Fawcett Columbine, 1982.

Campbell, Joseph. *The Hero with a Thousand Faces.* 2nd ed. Princeton, NJ: Princeton University Press, 1968.

Carre, John le. *Tinker, Tailor, Soldier, Spy.* New York: Knopf, 1974.

Code of Federal Regulations. U.S. Department of Agriculture, Title 9 (Animals and Animal Products) Chapter 1, Parts 1 to 3 (Animal Welfare), 1996. http://www.access.gpo.gov/nara/cfr/waisidx_99/9cfrv1_99.html (December 27, 2005).

Code of Federal Regulations. U.S. Department of Health and Human Services, Title 42 (Public Health) Part 72 (Additional Requirements for Facilities Transferring or Receiving Select Agents), 1996. http://www.cdc.gov/od/ohs/lrsat/42cfr72.htm (December 28, 2005).

Code of Federal Regulations. U.S. Department of Health and Human Services, Title 42 (Public Health), Part 93 (Research Misconduct), 2005a. http://ori.dhhs.gov/policies/regulations.shtml (December 30, 2005b).

Code of Federal Regulations. U.S. Department of Health and Human Services, Title 45 (Public Welfare), Part 46 (Protection of Human Subjects), 2005.http://www.hhs.gov/ohrp/humansubjects/guidance/45cfr46.htm#subparta (December 27, 2005a).

Committee on Institutional Cooperation. Urbana, IL.http://www.cic.uiuc.edu/ (January 1, 2006).

Council of Academic Deans From Research Education Institutions. Washington State University. Pullman, WA. http://www.cadrei.org/home.html (January 3, 2006).

Council of Colleges of Arts and Sciences. College of William and Mary. Williamsburg, VA. http://www.ccas.net/ (January 5, 2006).

Delaware Study. University of Delaware, National Study of Instructional Costs and Productivity. Newark, DE. http://www.udel.edu/IR/cost/ (January 20, 2006).

Diamond, Jared. *Guns, Germs, and Steel—The Fates of Human Societies.* New York: Norton, 1997.

Diversity Web. Association of American Colleges and Universities. http://
www.diversityweb.org/diversity_innovations/institutional_leadership/
index.cfm (October 16, 2005).

Engineering Dean's Council. American Association of Engineering Education.
Washington, DC. http://www.asee.org/members/organizations/
councils/edc.cfm (January 2, 2006).

The Faculty Room—Disabilities, Opportunities, Internetworking, and Technology.
University of Washington. Seattle, 2006.
http://www.washington.edu/doit/Faculty/ (January 4, 2006).

Fair Labor Standards Act (FLSA). U.S. Department of Labor. Washington, DC.
http://www.dol.gov/esa/whd/flsa/ (January 22, 2006).

Family Rights and Privacy Act (FERPA). U.S. Department of Education.
Washington, DC. http://www.ed.gov/policy/gen/guid/fpco/ferpa/
index.html (December 21, 2005).

Fausto-Sterling, Anne. *Sexing the Body: Gender Politics and the Construction of
Sexuality.* New York: Basic Books, 2000.

Field, Kelly. "U. of California Keeps Contract to Run Los Alamos Laboratory."
Chronicle of Higher Education 52, no. 18 (2006): A37.

Fredrickson, D. S. "A History of the Recombinant DNA Guidelines in the United
States." In *Recombinant DNA and Genetic Experimentation,* edited by
J. Morgan and W. J. Whelan. New York: Pergamon Press, 1979.

Friedman, Thomas L. *The World is Flat—A Brief History of the Twenty-First
Century.* New York: Farrar, Straus and Giroux, 2005.

Gaining Ground, Report of the 2010 Commission. Fayetteville: University of
Arkansas, 2005.

Gearhart, G. David. *Philanthropy, Fundraising, and the Capital Campaign.*
Washington, DC: National Association of College and University Business
Officers, 2006.

Gmelch, Walter H., and Val D. Miskin. *Chairing an Academic Department.* 2nd ed.
Madison, WI: Atwood Publishing, 2004.

Grossman, Paul D. "Making Accommodations: The Legal World of Students
with Disabilities." *Academe* (American Association of University Professors
Publications), 2001. http://www.aaup.org/publications/Academe/2001/
01nd/01ndgro.htm (January 4, 2006).

Guide for the Care and Use of Laboratory Animals. Washington, D. C.: National
Academy Press, 1996. http://www.nap.edu/readingroom/books/labrats/
(December 27, 2005).

Hewlett-Packard Website. *1940s:* http://www.hp.com/hpinfo/abouthp/
histnfacts/timeline/hist_40s.html (September 3, 2005).

IDEA (Individual Development and Educational Assessment) Center. Kansas
State University. Manhattan, KS. http://www.idea.ksu.edu/ (January 20,
2006).

IdeaBank. Rye, New York. http://www.idea-bank.com/ib/html/ (October 22,
2005).

Imagine. Inquire. Impart. A Final Report on the Campaign for the Twenty-First Century. Fayetteville: University of Arkansas, 2005.

Indiana University Purdue University Indianapolis. *Teaching for Student Success Module on Multicultural Teaching.* Indianapolis, IN. http://opd.iupui.edu/TSSS_modules/inclusive/introduction/1.htm (October 22, 2005).

Institute of Biological Engineering. Minneapolis, MN. http://www.ibeweb.org/ (January 3, 2006).

Institute of Electrical and Electronics Engineers. Piscataway, NJ. http://www.ieee.org/portal/site (January 3,2006).

Institute of Industrial Engineers. Norcross, GA. http://www.iienet.org/ (January 3, 2006).

International Association of Administrative Professionals (IAAP). Kansas City, MO. http://www.iaap-hq.org/ (November 22, 2005).

Jannarone, Anne. Center for Students with Disabilities. University of Arkansas, Fayetteville, AR, personal communication, 2005.

Kouzes, J. M., and B. Z. Posner. *The Leadership Challenge: How to Get Extraordinary Things Done in Organizations.* San Francisco: Jossey-Bass, 1989.

Kwiram, Alvin L. "An Overview on Indirect Costs." *Journal of Higher Education Strategists* 1 no.4, (2004): 387–436.

Lawrence Livermore National Laboratory. Livermore, CA. http://www.llnl.gov/ (January 8, 2006).

Lincoln Laboratory. Massachusetts Institute of Technology. Lexington, MA. http://www.ll.mit.edu/ (January 8, 2006).

LSU in the Eye of the Storm: A University Model for Disaster Response. DVD (six minutes). Baton Rouge: Louisiana State University, 2005.

Lucas, Ann E. *Strengthening Departmental Leadership—A Team-Building Guide for Chairs in Colleges and Universities.* San Francisco: Jossey-Bass, 1994.

Maimonides, Moses. *The Guide for the Perplexed.* Vols. 1 and 2. Translated by Shlomo Pines. 1190. Reprint, Chicago: University of Chicago Press, 1974.

Making the Case: The Impact of the University of Arkansas on the Future of the State of Arkansas, Report of the 2010 Commission. Fayetteville: University of Arkansas, 2001.

Mallard, Kina S. "Management by Walking Around and the Department Chair." *The Department Chair* 10 no. 2 (Fall 1999). http://www.uu.edu/centers/faculty/resources/article.cfm?ArticleID=230 (October 22, 2005).

Martin, Josef (pseudonym). *To Rise Above Principle—The Memoirs of an Unreconstructed Dean.* Urbana: University of Illinois Press, 1988.

McCray, Suzanne, ed. *Beyond Winning: National Scholarship Competitions and Student Experiences.* Fayetteville: University of Arkansas Press, 2005.

McFadden Allen, Barbara (CIC), and Lawrence Dumas (provost, Northwestern University), personal communications, 2005.

Middaugh, Michael F. "A Benchmarking Approach to Managing Instructional Costs and Enhancing Faculty Productivity." *Journal of Higher Education Strategists* 1 no.3, (2003): 221–41.

Mill, John Stuart. *A System of Logic.* 8th ed. New York: Harper, 1891.

The Minerals, Metals and Materials Society (TMS). Warrendale, PA, 2006. http://www.tms.org/TMSHome.html (January 3, 2006).

Model Policy for Responding to Allegations of Scientific Misconduct. Office of Research Integrity, U.S. Department of Health and Human Services, 1997. http://ori.dhhs.gov/policies/model_policy.shtml (December 30, 2005).

Model Procedures for Responding to Allegations of Scientific Misconduct. Office of Research Integrity, U.S. Department of Health and Human Services, 1997. http://ori.dhhs.gov/policies/model_policy.shtml (December 30, 2005).

Nasar, Sylvia. *A Beautiful Mind.* New York: Simon and Shuster, 1998.

National Association of Independent Colleges and Universities. Washington, DC. http://www.naicu.edu/ (January 20, 2006).

National Association of State Universities and Land-Grant Colleges. Washington, DC. http://www.nasulgc.org/ (January 2, 2006).

National Center for Educational Statistics. U.S. Department of Education. Washington, DC. http://nces.ed.gov/pubsearch/pubsinfo.asp?pubid=2003161 (January 20, 2006).

National Institutes of Health. *Guidelines for Research Involving Recombinant DNA Molecules.* Bethesda, MD, 2002. http://www4.od.nih.gov/oba/rac/guidelines/guidelines.html (December 28, 2005).

National Institutes of Health. Office of Laboratory Animal Welfare, U.S. Department of Health and Human Services, Bethesda, MD. http://grants.nih.gov/grants/olaw/olaw.htm#gen (December 27, 2005).

National Weather Service (National Oceanic and Atmospheric Administration). Washington, DC. http://www.nws.noaa.gov/ (January 12, 2006).

Newman, Joanna L., and Anne M. O'Leary-Kelly. *Diversity and Faculty Experiences: A Survey of the University of Arkansas Campus.* Fayetteville: University of Arkansas, 2003 (and parallel reports on staff and students). http://advancement.uark.edu/diversity/ (October 16, 2005).

Now is the Time—Meeting the Challenge for a Diverse Academy. Report of the National Association of State University and Land-Grant Colleges (NASULGC)–American Association of State Colleges and Universities (AASCU) Task Force on Diversity. Washington, DC. NASULGC, 2005. http://www.nasulgc.org/initiatives.htm (November 8, 2005).

On This Day. New York: New York Times. http://www.nytimes.com/learning/general/onthisday/ (October 23, 2005).

Picking Up the Pace, Report of the 2010 Commission. Fayetteville: University of Arkansas, 2004.

Ratcliff, James L., Edward S. Lubinescu, and Maureen A. Gaffney, eds. *How Accreditation Influences Assessment: New Directions for Higher Education.* San Francisco: Jossey-Bass, 2001.

Rosovsky, Henry. *The University—An Owner's Manual.* New York: Norton, 1990.

Rutledge, Reynie, and Bob Smith. "Arkansas Included—The Roles and Benefits of Research Universities." *All Things Academic* 1, no. 3), November 2000. http://libinfo.uark.edu/ata/ (December 7, 2005.)

———. "Arkansas in Context—How Arkansas and the University of Arkansas Compare." *All Things Academic* 1 no. 3, November 2000. http://libinfo.uark.edu/ata/ (December 7, 2005).

———. "Advancing the State's Flagship University—Challenges Posed by Recent Higher Education Initiatives in Arkansas." *All Things Academic* 1, no. 3, November 2000. http://libinfo.uark.edu/ata/ (December 7, 2005).

———. "Making a Difference in Arkansas and the World—The Role of Higher Education in Society." *All Things Academic* 1, no.3, November 2000. http://libinfo.uark.edu/ata/ (December 7, 2005).

———. "More to Come—Progress at the University of Arkansas." *All Things Academic,* 1 no. 3, November, 2000. http://libinfo.uark.edu/ata/ (December 7, 2005).

Sagan, Carl, *The Dragons of Eden—Speculations on the Evolution of Human Intelligence.* New York: Ballantine Books, 1977 (reissue edition, 1986).

Saint-Exupéry, Antoine de. *The Little Prince.* Translated by Katherine Woods. New York: Harcourt, Brace and World, 1943.

Sample, Steven B. *The Contrarian's Guide to Leadership.* San Francisco: Jossey-Bass, 2002.

Seagren, Alan T., John W. Creswell, and Daniel W. Wheeler. *The Department Chair—New Roles, Responsibilities and Challenges.* Washington, DC: George Washington University, 1993 and references cited therein.

Securing America's Future: Global Education for a Global Age. (Report on the Strategic Task Force on Study Abroad). Paul Simon and Richard W. Riley, Co-Chairs. Washington, DC: NAFSA—Association of International Educators, 2003.

Small Business Innovation Research (SBIR) and Small Business Technology Transfer (STTR) Programs. National Institutes of Health, Office of Extramural Research. Bethesda, MD, 2005. http://grants.nih.gov/grants/funding/sbirsttr_programs.htm (December 30, 2005).

Smith, Bob. "How Does One Happen to Become a Provost?" *All Things Academic* 4, no. 3, October 2003. http://libinfo.uark.edu/ata/ (September 9, 2005).

———. "The Integrated Scholar—Have You Seen One Lately?" *All Things Academic* 4, no. 1, February 2002. http://libinfo.uark.edu/ata/ (February 1, 2006).

———. "The Integrated Scholar—Once More Once." *All Things Academic* 5 no. 3, September 2004. http://libinfo.uark.edu/ata/ (February 1, 2006).

———. "In Search of Integrated Scholars, Part IV." *All Things Academic* 6 no.3, September 2005. http://libinfo.uark.edu/ata/ (February 1, 2006).

———. "The Integrated Scholar Revisited." *All Things Academic* 4, no. 3, October 2003. http://libinfo.uark.edu/ata/ (February 1, 2006).

Smith, Bob, and Don Pederson. "Academic Program Efficiency and Assessment." *All Things Academic.* 2 no. 4, November, 2001. http://libinfo.uark.edu/ata/ (December 12, 2005).

Smith, Daryl G., Lisa E. Wolf, and Bonnie E. Busenberg. *Achieving Faculty*

Diversity: Debunking the Myths. Washington, DC: Association American Colleges and Universities, 1996.

Smith, Robert V. *Development and Management of University Research Groups.* 2nd ed. Austin: University of Texas Press, 1986.

———. *The Elements of Great Speechmaking—Adding Drama and Intrigue.* Lanham, MD: University Press of America, 2004.

———. *Graduate Research—A Guide for Students in the Sciences.* 3rd ed. Seattle: University of Washington Press, 1998.

———. *Pedestals, Parapets and Pits—The Joys, Challenges and Failures of Professional Life.* Fayetteville, AR: Phoenix International, 2005.

Southeastern Conference Academic Consortium Report on Study Abroad Initiative. Fayetteville, AR: Office of the Provost, University of Arkansas, 2005.

Southeastern Universities Research Association (SURA). Washington, DC. http://www1.sura.org/0000/0000_Home.html (January 8, 2006).

Spangehl, Stephen D. "The North Central Association of Colleges and Schools Academic Quality Improvement Project (AQIP)." In *Pursuing Excellence in Higher Education: Eight Fundamental Challenges,* edited by Brent D. Ruben. San Francisco: Jossey-Bass, 2004.

Thoreau, Henry David. *Walden.* 1854. Reprint, New York: Bantam Books, 1962.

Tucker, Allan. *The Academic Dean: Dove, Dragon, and Diplomat.* Toronto: Macmillan, 1991.

Tucker, Allan. *Chairing the Academic Department.* 3rd ed. Phoenix: Oryx Press, 1993 and references cited therein.

Turner, Caroline Sotello Viernes. *Diversifying the Faculty: A Guidebook for Search Committees.* Washington, DC: Association American Colleges and Universities, 2002.

University of Arkansas. Academic Policy Series (1435.70). *Faculty Salary Funding Incentive Plan.* http://www.uark.edu/admin/vcacsey/AcaPolicySeries/academic_policies.html. (October 8, 2005).

University of Arkansas. Academic Policy Series (1407.20). *Guidelines for Fifth-Year Review of Deans.* http://www.uark.edu/admin/vcacsey/AcaPolicySeries/academic_policies.html. (December 18, 2005).

University of Arkansas Campus Council Document. February 13, 1992. *Conflicts of Interest and Commitment.* http://www.uark.edu/admin/rsspinfo/compliance/conduct/index.html (December 29, 2005)

University of Arkansas Faculty Handbook. Section Two, Academic Responsibilities of Faculty. August 15, 2005. http://www.uark.edu/admin/vcacsey/facultyhandbook/ (December 29, 2005).

University of North Carolina at Chapel Hill. *Diversity in the College Classroom.* http://www.unc.edu/depts/ctl/tfitoc.html (October 22, 2005).

University of Wisconsin-Madison. Equity and Diversity Virtual Resource Center. http://www.library.wisc.edu/EDVRC/improvingcampusclimate.html (October 22, 2005).

U.S. Department of Homeland Security. Washington, DC. http://www.dhs.gov/dhspublic/ (December 28, 2005).

U.S. Drug Enforcement Administration. Washington, DC. http://www.usdoj.gov/dea/ (December 28, 2005).

U.S. Environmental Protection Agency. Washington, DC. http://www.epa.gov/ (December 28, 2005).

U.S. Equal Employment Opportunities Commission. *Facts About Sexual Harassment*. http://www.eeoc.gov/facts/fs-sex.html (December 30, 2005).

U.S. Equal Employment Opportunity Commission. Washington, DC. http://www.eeoc.gov/ (January 22, 2006).

U.S. Nuclear Regulatory Commission. Washington, DC. http://www.nrc.gov/ (December 28, 2005).

U.S. Office of Research Integrity. U.S. Department of Health and Human Services. Rockville, MD. http://ori.dhhs.gov/ (January 22, 2006).

Wells, Herman B. "A Case Study on Interinstitutional Cooperation." *Educational Record* (American Council on Education), Fall 1967. http://www.cic.uiuc.edu/AboutCIC.shtml (December 31, 2005).

Western Commission for Higher Education. Boulder, CO. http://www.wiche.edu/ (January 8, 2006).

Wilder, Thornton. *Our Town*. 1938. Reprint, New York: HarperCollins, 2003.

Wilson, Edward O. *Consilience—The Unity of Knowledge*. New York: Knopf, 1998.

Wilson, Robin. "The Murder of a Professor—A Failed Graduate Student Kills the Scholar Who Gave Him a Second Chance at a Ph.D." *Chronicle of Higher Education,* on-line edition. September 15, 2000. http://chronicle.com/weekly/v47/i03/03a01401.htm (October 30, 2005).

Wit, Hans de. *Internationalization of Higher Education in the United States of America and Europe: A Historical, Comparative, and Conceptual Analysis.* New York: Greenwood Press, 2002.

Wolverton, Mimi, Walter H. Gmelch, Joni Montez, and Charles T. Nies. *The Changing Nature of the Academic Deanship.* San Francisco: Jossey Bass, 2001.

Woods, Randall Bennett. *Fulbright—A Biography.* New York: Cambridge University Press, 1995.

World Factbook. U.S. Central Intelligence Agency. Washington, DC. http://www.odci.gov/cia/publications/factbook/index.html (October 23, 2005).

Zimbler, Linda J. *Background Characteristics, Work Activities, and Compensation of Faculty and Instructional Staff in Postgraduate Institutions.* NCES Publication 2001152. Washington, DC: U.S. Department of Education, National Center for Education Statistics, 2001. http://nces.ed.gov/pubsearch/pubsinfo.asp?pubid=2001152 (January 21, 2006).

Index

Internet, 4, 60, 87, 180; courses, 87; internationalization and, 180; interviews, 4; resources, 60; use, 4, 60
interpersonal interactions, 11–12

interview, 4
intrapreneurs, 39–45; faculty and staff, 39–45
Iraq. *See* Baghdad
Irish coast, 62
Irish studies, 181. *See also* international outreach
James E. Bauerle Professorship, 45. *See also* University of Texas at Austin
Jannarone, Anne. *See* University of Arkansas
Janus, 60
jealousy, 70
Johns Hopkins University, 177. *See also* Applied Physics Laboratory
journalist. *See* Murrow, Edward R.
Journal of Chemical Education, 37
journals, 7, 9, 13, 17, 21, 27, 32, 36–37, 78, 119; chemistry, 37; communication, 37; education, 21; on-line, 7, 17, 27, 78, 119; peer-reviewed, 36; professional, 21; top-tier, 37. See also *All Things Academic; Communication Education; Journal of Chemical Education; Women of Note*
joys of academic life, 65–67, 69, 71, 200. *See also* pedestals of academic life
Jung, Carl, 29

Kansas, 26
Katrina hurricane, 75–76. *See also* Louisiana State University
Kelly, James Easton, 72. *See also* University of Arkansas
Kettering, Charles. *See* quotes
King, Martin Luther, Jr., 48
King Minos, 57
Kriegspiel, the game of, 105
K-12, 1, 41, 186; funding priorities and, 41; inclement weather and, 186
Kupchik, Eugene, 24

Lahr, Bert, 61. See also *Wizard of Oz, The*
languages, myriad. *See* diversity
lapel pins, 64–65. *See also* sartorial accessories
Larson, Gary, xvii; "Be weird," xvii; "Far Side," xvii
Latin America, 25

Lawrence Livermore National Laboratory, 177. *See also* partnerships with academic, corporate, government, and non-government organizations; University of California Berkeley
leadership development, xv, 6, 85–86, 87, 98, 103, 166–67; associate and vice chairs, 103; Committee on Institutional Cooperation and, 166; faculty, xv, 86, 166; Southeastern Conference Academic Consortium and, 167
Le Carré, John, 58. *See also* Matryoshka dolls; Talburt, Nancy; *Tinker, Tailor, Soldier, Spy*
liberal arts, 47–48, 112–13, 115; curriculum, 113; diversity and, 47–48; educated professionals and, 48; hypothetical college of, 115; Middlebury College and, 112–13; mission statements and, 112–13; St. John's University and, 113
Lichtenstein, Roy, 110. *See also* strategic planning
lifelong learning, 67, 104–5, 113–14
Lincoln, Abraham, 60, 109. *See also* quotes
Lincoln Laboratory, 177. *See also* Massachusetts Institute of Technology
listening and listening skills, 1, 4, 10–13, 15, 67; artful, 10–12; being truly present, 11; communications with supervisor, 10; meetings and, 15; pedestal of professional life, 67. *See also* interpersonal interactions
Little Prince, The, 57, 189–90. *See also* Saint-Exupéry, Antoine de
living mosaic. *See* diversity
Locke, John, 73. *See also* University of Arkansas
Long Island Sound, 62
Los Alamos Laboratories, 177. *See also* partnerships with academic, corporate, government, and non-government organizations
lottery, 29
Louisiana, 26, 62, 75, 120, 166, 184. *See also* Louisiana State University; Natchitoches, Louisiana
Louisiana State University, 26, 75–76; Katrina hurricane, 75–76. *See also* Emmert, Mark
loyalty, 104
Luongo, Hugh, 23
lust, 70

About the Author

Bob Smith has crafted a career serving U.S. higher education—as faculty member; academic division head; assistant director, associate director, and director of a research institute; dean of a professional college; dean of two graduate schools; interim dean of an honors college; chief research officer (vice provost) at two institutions; and chief academic officer (provost and vice chancellor for academic affairs)—at the universities of Arkansas, Iowa, Texas at Austin, and Connecticut (UConn), along with Washington State University. Currently, he is serving as provost and vice-chancellor for academic affairs at the University of Arkansas in Fayetteville. He holds MS and PhD degrees from the University of Michigan where he has since been recognized as one of fifty Distinguished Doctoral Graduates of the Horace H. Rackham School of Graduate Studies (1987) and Distinguished Alumnus of the College of Pharmacy (1990).

Bob is the author or coauthor of over 270 publications and eight books, including *Graduate Research—A Guide for Students in the Sciences, The Elements of Great Speechmaking—Add Drama and Intrigue,* and *Pedestals, Parapets & Pits—The Joys, Challenges and Failures of Professional Life.* During his career, Bob has served on many boards (e.g., Council of Graduate Schools Board of Directors, Graduate Record Exam Board, Washington Research Foundation Board of Directors) and executive committees (e.g., Executive Committee of Graduate Deans of the Africa-America Institute). He has also served as a consultant to universities and private industry, including Rutgers University, the University of Utah, and Wayne State University, Hoechst-Roussel Pharmaceuticals, Hoffmann-LaRoche, E. R. Squibb and Sons, and the Upjohn Company.

Bob lives on the Ozark Plateau in Fayetteville with his artist wife, Marsha June, and their French bulldogs Monsieur Hercule Poirot, Mademoiselle Millicent Le Fay, and Monsieur Maurice Chevalier Le Bat.